D0325148

THE CHILDREN'S MATERIAL

A Complete "Miracles" Course for Children

THE CHILDREN'S MATERIAL

A Complete "Miracles" Course for Children

Bette Jean Cundiff

Miracle Distribution Center
1998

Interior Illustrations by
Kelvin Nguyen

Cover and book design by
Steve Doolittle

Published by:

MIRACLE DISTRIBUTION CENTER
1141 E. Ash Ave.
Fullerton, CA 92831
(714)738-8380
www.miraclecenter.org

Previous Publishing History

Miracle Experiences and You Publishing:
(Former ISBN 1-880436-02-7)

Third Printing - 1980
Fourth Printing 1987
Fifth Printing 1989
Sixth Printing 1992
Seventh Printing 1996

ISBN 0-9618309-1-3

To Christine, Shawn and David—my children and my teachers

Author's Note:

These words were sent from the One Teacher Who guides us all.

May His words shine from the pages of this book, through the clouds of fear, to join with the inner brightness of your soul.

May each of us hear His Word and then spread His message through the loving demonstration of our lives.

May you always be aware
of His presence.

CONTENTS

PART I

Little Lamb: The Miracle Fables

PART II

The Children's Workbook

PART III

Instructions for Working with Children

PART IV

Help Is On The Way:
Miracles Course for Slightly Older Children

PART I

Little Lamb
The Miracle Fables

OUR FATHER'S WORLD

God's world was everywhere and everything. God's world was filled with love and beauty. God's world was filled with the music of happiness. The bubbling brooks laughed happily. The sunlight danced and flickered. The trees rustled their contentment.

Little Lamb was at peace in his Father's world. Here was warm sunlight, cool water to drink and green grass to eat. Here all the animals lived in love and brotherhood. Their Father was in them and around them. He spoke to them in their hearts.

One day God called to Little Lamb, "Little Lamb, I need your help."

"Yes, Father," answered Little Lamb, "How can I help you?"

And his Father said, "Little Lamb, you are perfect and loving just as all My children are. And when My children are awake in My world they can see their perfection for I love all My children and have created them this way. But sometimes My children sleep. And when they sleep they dream and in their dreams they forget My love. They forget they are perfect. They forget their Father Who is with them always and Who loves them.

"You, Little Lamb, understand this and can see the love in all your brothers. Now you must sleep and dream too. Dream Little Lamb, but in your dreams remember Me. And help your brothers to remember Me also. Teach them that the world they think they see is but a dream. Help them awaken and open their eyes to My real world for here is love and happiness."

And Little Lamb was filled with the wonder and peace of God's love. "Yes, Father. I will sleep and I will dream. But I will remember that You are with me always. I will go into the dream world and help all my brothers to remember You and awake into Your real world."

As the sun gently dipped below the trees Little Lamb curled into a comfortable ball. The music of the birds and insects softly sang a lullaby to soothe Little Lamb to sleep. And in his heart he heard his Father's words. "You are My Son in whom I am well pleased. Your work has begun. Dream sweet dreams, Little Lamb. And in your dreams awaken My children so they may remember My love for them."

FROM FEAR TO LOVE

Little Lamb opened his eyes slowly. Carefully he climbed to his feet. "Learn, enjoy and teach. There is much for you to do," came God's Voice in his heart.

"Quickly, come quickly Little Lamb. We need your help." Within the dream Little Lamb opened his eyes. Around him were the animals of the forest. Mouse was scurrying here and there. Raccoon moved out of sight behind a tree stump.

"You must help us Little Lamb," said Mouse. Fear kept twitching his whiskers. "There is something awful in the forest and you must save us." Raccoon moved further behind the tree stump hoping no one would see him.

"Have you looked to see what it is?" asked Little Lamb. "The fear in your hearts will go away when you know what it is you fear."

Mouse looked at Raccoon and twitched his whiskers angrily. Raccoon slunk further behind the stump. "We are too afraid to look."

Little Lamb's heart went out to his friends. He knew he must discover what hid in the darkness of the forest for fear disappears in the light of love. And so off he went, fearless in his Father's love.

As darkness began to fall, Little Lamb walked deeper into the forest. His friends were far behind him. Deeper and deeper he went. The blackness covered him and he felt alone. He had forgotten his Father would be with him always.

Separated from his friends in a part of the forest he did not know, Little Lamb became afraid. The snap of a branch near him made Little Lamb jump with fright. Now he seemed to be surrounded by rustling and crackling. Little Lamb's heart pounded in his chest.

"Oh why am I here?" And as quickly as he had asked the question, the answer came. Softly and gently the words rose from his heart. "You are in the dream world Little Lamb and you came to help your friends awaken because you love them as I love you."

Then Little Lamb knew he was not alone, for his Father was within him. Fear left Little Lamb, and in its place came peace and happiness for he could feel his Father's love.

For the first time Little Lamb looked up and saw the moon shining through the trees. So brightly did it shine that he could see around him as if it were day. And there, hiding behind a large bush, was an animal. His coat was golden yellow. A large mane of fur circled his face. It was a lion.

“Hello Lion,” called Little Lamb. As he spoke he noticed tears falling from Lion’s eyes. Gently Little Lamb asked, “Can I help you?”

“I am so lonely and frightened. Each time I come near anyone to say hello, they run away.”

Little Lamb smiled. So this was what Mouse and Raccoon feared. It was only Lion, lonely and frightened just as they were. “Come, do not be afraid. Let us be friends and through me you will meet the friends for whom you search.”

As Little Lamb and Lion came out of the woods into the clearing, Mouse, whiskers twitching, ran behind a boulder. Raccoon scurried under a fern, eyes large and frightened.

“Come. Don’t be afraid,” called Little Lamb to his friends.

“Lion was alone in the forest and needs our friendship as much as we need his. Come and meet what frightened you. For he is the same as you. Lonely and frightened he reaches out for your friendship. Can you say ‘no’ to him?”

And so Mouse and Raccoon slowly came forward. As the animals’ fear began to disappear, friendship and love took its place.

Little Lamb could hear his Father’s Voice speak to all of them in their hearts. “Today you chose love instead of fear. For without fear, there could only be love.”

Mouse said, “Thank you Little Lamb for teaching us to look through fear to the love that is always there, waiting for us to reach out and accept it.” With that Mouse reached out his hand and took Lion’s paw. Fear had disappeared and only love remained in all of them.

OUR FATHER'S VOICE

Little Lamb remembered his Father's words. He would go deep within the dream world and awaken all those who were asleep and had forgotten their Father's world. Darkness, as soft as a blanket, covered Little Lamb and in his sleep he began to dream. And in the dream he was on a path in a forest.

Gray Squirrel was scampering back and forth under a large tree, its leaves a bright orange.

"Hello Gray Squirrel. How are you this fine day?" asked Little Lamb.

"Terrible, terrible. That's how I am this fine Fall day. Soon the frost will be coming and then the snow. The snow will cover all the nuts and seeds and pollynoses. What shall I eat then? Oh dear, what shall I do?" And off the squirrel ran.

Little Lamb walked further down the path in the forest and there he met Bear. "Hello Bear. How are you this fine day?" asked Little Lamb.

Bear looked down sadly at Little Lamb and sighed. "The long winter is coming and I am a big bear. I am always hungry. How will I be able to live through the winter when the snow comes and the bees stop making honey for me to eat?" Bear walked slowly into the woods sighing deeply to himself.

Again Little Lamb walked further down the path. Over his head flew a flock of geese, their wings flapping loudly. "Where are you going on such a fine day?" asked Little Lamb.

"Where, oh where, can we go?" asked the largest goose. "Soon the winter will come and the lakes will freeze and the trees will be covered with snow. Where will we live without freezing?" And off the geese flew squawking unhappily.

Little Lamb sat down on the side of the path. He was troubled by his friends' problems. He knew he must help them, but how? And so, Little Lamb closed his eyes and within his heart he asked his Father for help. "Father, my friends are worried and frightened. They need Your help. What can I do?"

And through the mist of the dream his Father's Voice answered him. "Tell your friends, Little Lamb, that I will listen to their questions and answer them. All they must do is ask and then listen for My answer within their hearts. I love all My children and I am always here to help them."

And so Little lamb called all the animals together and told them, "Our Father, Who is always with us will help you. All you must do is close your

eyes, ask for His help and listen to your hearts. He will answer."

Gray Squirrel closed his eyes and said, "Father, I am worried. Soon the snow will cover all the nuts and seeds. How will I eat?" And then Gray Squirrel sat quietly and listened to his heart.

"Do not worry Squirrel," came his Father's Voice. "Go and gather up all the nuts and seeds you can find. Store them in the ground. Then when the winter comes you can dig them up. This way you will never be hungry."

"Thank you Father. Now I know just what to do." And off scampered Gray Squirrel eager and happy to collect his nuts for the winter.

Bear closed his eyes and said, "Father, I am a big bear and am always hungry. I will starve this winter when the bees stop making honey. What shall I do?" And Bear sat quietly and listened to his heart.

"Do not worry Bear," came his Father's Voice, "Go to the honeycomb now and eat and eat. Grow very fat Bear, and then when you sleep all winter your food will be stored in your body and you will not be hungry."

"Thank you Father. Now I know just what to do." And off Bear went to eat honey and grow fat.

The largest goose closed his eyes and said, "Father, I must take care of my flock of geese. Where can we go when the lakes are frozen and the trees are full of snow?" And Goose sat quietly and listened to his heart.

"Do not worry Goose," came his Father's Voice. "Take your flock and fly far to the south. There it will stay warm all winter and there you will find lakes to swim on and leafy branches to sit on."

"Thank you Father. Now I know just what to do." And off flew the flock of geese toward the South.

Little Lamb smiled. He had helped his friends. Now they knew they must only ask and then listen for their Father's loving Voice. For in their Father's love was the answer to all their questions.

"You have done well today, my Son, came his Father's Voice. With that Little Lamb opened his eyes. He had been dreaming and now he was awake in God's world. And Little Lamb was happy.

WE ARE ALL OUR FATHER'S CHILDREN

Little Lamb was in the dream world. He was with all the animals of the forest. The warm evening breezes touched them gently as they sat and listened to Little Lamb speak.

Miss Rabbit moved forward shyly, and quietly asked Little Lamb, "You tell us that we are all brothers and sisters. But I don't understand. I have long ears, a fuzzy body and strong legs to hop with. Mr. and Mrs. Swan have long necks, feathers, wings to fly with and webbed feet to swim with. How can we be sisters and brothers?"

Then Owl spoke up, "Yes, Little Lamb, how can I be a brother to Miss Deer? I sleep all day and am awake all night, and she sleeps all night and is awake all day."

Bear spoke loudly in his deep voice, "Look at how big I am and how small Mouse is. How could we be brothers?"

Little Lamb smiled lovingly at his friends and said to Miss Rabbit "What do your mother and father look like?"

And Miss Rabbit said, "Why they have long ears, a fuzzy body and strong legs just like me."

"Tell me Owl," asked Little Lamb, "What are your parents like?"

And Owl thought for a moment and said, "You know, they sleep all day and are awake all night, just like me."

Then Little Lamb turned to Bear and said, "Your father must be big, just like you." And Bear nodded his head to answer "Yes."

"You are all your parents' children. You look like them and you act like them. Now tell me who is the Father of everyone and everything?"

And all the animals smiled and said together, "God is the Father of everyone and everything."

"Now tell me what God our Father is like."

Bear said loudly, "He is all powerful."

Owl said thoughtfully, "He is very wise and knows everything."

Miss Rabbit blushed and quietly said, "He is our Father and loves us."

Little Lamb asked his friends, "Can you see God our Father?"

And Miss Deer looked up and said, "God is in our hearts. He isn't something you ***see***, God is love and that is something you can only ***feel***."

Now Little Lamb looked at all his friends and said, "God our Father is powerful, and wise and loving. And He is always in our hearts ready to help us. Now think for a moment. You are your parents' children and as your parents are, so are you also. If God is in all of your hearts, then you must be in all of your brothers' and sisters' hearts also. If God is always ready to help us and love us, then we are always ready to help and love each other. For God is our Father and we are like Him."

Owl's eyes lit up and he said, "Now I understand. Our bodies are just costumes we put on for fun. They help us do our jobs. But it is what's inside that is real. That is where God is. And where God our Father is, so our brothers and sisters are also. They are in our hearts always."

Little Lamb smiled and all the animals smiled at each other. In their hearts they could hear their Father's Voice saying, "'You are all My children: powerful, wise and always loving for I have made you so."

And as the soft moonlight shone on all of them, they could feel in their hearts that they were truly brothers and sisters. They were one.

FORGIVENESS

Little Lamb closed his eyes and quickly fell asleep. He must enter the dream again for there was more work for him to do.

Two chipmunks were making a horrible noise in the grassy clearing. Both the chipmunks were chattering in anger. Bits of grass began to fly as the two began to nip and scratch each other.

"You always find the biggest nuts and never let me have any," screeched Little Chipmunk.

"That's right," yelled back the other.
"Whenever I find any nuts you steal them away for yourself." And back to fighting they went. Bits of fur and grass flying into the air.

Little Lamb walked into the clearing. "My brothers, what could be making you so angry?"

Big Chipmunk stopped nipping Little Chipmunk and said, "Every day I get up very early and work hard gathering nuts to eat. And every night when I am fast asleep he comes and steals them. This is not fair."

Little Chipmunk looked up at Little Lamb, tears of hurt and anger in

his eyes. "Big Chipmunk never shares his nuts with me. Every day we go out to search for nuts to eat. And every day he finds the biggest and the most. I am much smaller than he is. I cannot run as fast so I cannot find them first. I am not as strong so I cannot carry as many as he can. I am always hungry and never have enough to eat. While he always has more than enough to eat. This is not fair. So when Big Chipmunk is not looking

I steal some of his nuts for myself."

Little Lamb looked at both the chipmunks. He could see the fear each of them had in his heart.

He could see that it was this fear that was making them angry with each other.

"Brothers," said Little Lamb, "You both were afraid you would not have enough to eat. You both were selfish and forgot to look at your brother with love. You felt fear and anger and gave that to your brother, and that is what he gave back to you. Now let us try to see only the good and the love in each other...for surely that is what we will get in return."

Big Chipmunk looked down at Little Chipmunk and said, "If you were always hungry, and I always had enough to eat, why didn't you ask me for some extra nuts? Surely I would have given you some.

Little Chipmunk looked up at Big Chipmunk and said, I was afraid you would not give me any. You always seemed so angry with me."

"Yes, I was angry because I thought you were a thief. But now I can see you were just hungry and frightened, frightened you would not have enough to eat and frightened of me." Both Chipmunks looked at each other with new eyes.

"Truly," said Little Lamb "Anger only comes from fear. And if you but look and listen to your brother with love the fear and then the anger will disappear."

"From now on," said Big Chipmunk, "We will search for nuts together. You can help me find them and I can help you carry them."

"Then we can share them together," said Little Chipmunk. And off they ran together, happy to be friends and not enemies.

Little Lamb smiled for he could hear his Father's Voice in his heart saying, "Your brothers forgave each other for they saw the truth: Anger comes from fear and fear disappears when love is shared."

With that Little Lamb opened his eyes and the mist of the dream cleared. He was back in his Father's world of love, peace and happiness.

THE CHOICE

Little Lamb entered the dream world again. His work was not finished as long as his brothers still forgot the real world of God.

Little Lamb and Beaver walked together through the forest. The sun shone brightly through the trees.

"The sun is very bright," said Beaver. He could feel the heat of the sun on the top of his head and thought: The sun is always too hot. When I am hot I feel tired. And when I am tired I feel grumpy. The sun is always too hot.

While Beaver thought his thoughts, Little Lamb was thinking also: How wonderfully warm and nice is the sun. Look how bright and beautiful it makes the forest. Thank you, Father, for letting me see the beauty of the sun.

Little Lamb and Beaver continued down the path in the forest. Soon they became hungry and began to look for something to eat. Beaver thought: Every time I am hungry I must look for food to eat. I must dig in the dirt for roots. I must always work. And when I work I feel tired. And when I am tired I feel grumpy.

Little Lamb also thought: Look at all this nice green grass to eat. Look at all the roots in the ground for my friend to eat. How wonderful is God Who gives us all we need. Thank you, Father.

After the friends had eaten, they grew tired and decided to rest. As Beaver lay on the ground he thought: Listen to all those insects buzzing. Listen to all those birds chirping. What an awful noise. How will I be able to rest if I must listen to this racket?

Little Lamb also lay down to rest and he thought: Listen to my brothers, the insects, buzzing. Listen to my brothers, the birds, chirping. How beautiful are the songs of life. Thank you, Father, for sending me such a wonderful lullaby.

Later in the day Little Lamb and Beaver met another beaver by a stream.

"Please help," asked the other beaver. "This log is too big for me to lift by myself and I must put it in the stream to help build my house."

As Little Lamb and Beaver helped their brother lift the log Beaver thought: Look at all this work I must do now. The log is getting my fur dirty and the water of the stream is making me wet and cold. And when I am dirty and wet and cold I get grumpy.

Little Lamb was also thinking as he helped his brother: How cool the water is as it washes the dirt off my wool. How nice it is to help my brother. Thank you, Father, for giving me this chance to help a friend, and for giving me the gift of my friend's thankful smile.

Later that evening Beaver heard Little Lamb saying, Thank you, Father, for a most beautiful and happy day."

"How can you say this day was beautiful and happy?" exclaimed Beaver. "The sun was too hot. It was hard to find food to eat. The noise of the birds and insects kept me awake, and I got dirty and wet and cold lifting that log."

"But don't you see that is how you decided to see the day," said Little Lamb. "Now listen to how I saw the day: The sun was warm and beautiful. The grass was sweet and plentiful. The birds and insects sang me a lullaby and our brother gave us the gift of his loving smile. And for all this I am very thankful."

Beaver's eyes began to light up. "You know Little Lamb, it wasn't what I did today, but how I decided to look at it. I chose to see only unhappiness in all that we did, and I was grumpy and unhappy. You chose to see only happiness in all that we did, and you were happy."

"Now you see," said Little Lamb smiling, "You decided whether to be happy or not. God our Father gives us only love and goodness. It is up to us to decide if we want to see that love and goodness."

And as Beaver looked around him he saw the shining stars and felt the warm night breeze as soft as a blanket on his fur and said, "Thank you, Father, for this beautiful night." And Beaver and Little Lamb smiled.

HAPPINESS

Little Lamb walked through the mist of the dream. His brothers were waiting for him. They had questions for him to answer.

Little Lamb sat in the center of the circle. All his brothers who lived in the forest sat around him and listened.

"'Little Lamb," called one of the animals, "Tell us about happiness."

Little Lamb looked at all his friends and smiled, "First let me ask you what you think happiness is."

Gray Squirrel looked at Little Lamb and said, "Happiness is having piles and piles of seeds and nuts. When I have all the seeds and nuts in the world, then I will be happy."

"Are you happy now?" asked Little Lamb.

"No," said Gray Squirrel. "But I will be when I get all the seeds and nuts in the world."

Fat Robin with tears in her eyes said, "I just lost happiness. This past summer all my babies were with me as I helped them grow big and strong. Now they are gone to have their own families and with them went my happiness."

"Are you happy now?" asked Little Lamb.

"No," said Fat Robin. "When my children were with me I had

happiness, but now they are gone and my happiness is gone also."

Pack Rat spoke up next. In his arms he held all the odd things he had found that day: a stone, an acorn and a small tin can. "I am happy when I have with me all the things that I find. It took me a long time to find these things. I won't let anybody take them from me. As long as I have them I am happy."

"Are you happy now?" asked Little Lamb.

"Now I am happy because I have all my things. But I am afraid that I will lose them." And so Pack Rat sat down clutching his things close to him, frightened that he would lose his happiness.

Little Lamb looked at his friends and said, "Gray Squirrel is not happy now because he has not found happiness yet. Fat Robin is not happy now because she has just lost happiness. Pack Rat thinks he is happy because he has all his things, but he is frightened that he will lose them. So if he is frightened, can he really be happy?"

And Pack Rat said, I guess I am not really happy because I am afraid I will lose those things that I thought were happiness. Tell us, Little Lamb, how we can be happy now."

Little Lamb smiled at his brothers and said, "Happiness is not something, or someone, or someplace. Happiness just is, inside you. When you feel God's love in your heart you feel happy. When you want to share God's love with all your brothers you feel happy. And when you feel happy inside your happiness shines on everyone you meet. When you feel happy inside no matter who you are with, where you are or what you have, you will be happy because you carry it around with you."

"Are you happy now, Gray Squirrel?" asked Little Lamb.

"Yes, I am happy. It's not the nuts and seeds that will make me happy, only me," said the squirrel.

"Are you happy now, Fat Robin?" asked Little Lamb.

"Yes, I am happy, because I love my children whether they are with me or not," said Fat Robin.

"Are you happy now, Pack Rat?" asked Little Lamb.

"Yes, I am happy, because if I am happy inside myself it doesn't matter if I have my things or lose my things, I will still be happy."

And as they all sat in the circle, God's love was in them and around them and they were all very happy.

LOVE

Little Lamb walked through the mist of the dream and came upon a lovely pond. Two swans began to swim toward him.

"Hello, Little Lamb," said Mr. Swan. "I would like you to meet my new wife whom I love very much." Mrs. Swan smiled sweetly at Little Lamb.

"Hello, Mr. and Mrs. Swan," said Little Lamb. "You. both seem very happy together."

"Yes, we are happy," said the swan, "because we love each other.

Little Lamb smiled at his friends and asked, "Can you tell me why you love each other?"

Mr. Swan laughed and said, "That is easy, it is because my wife is so pretty." And Mrs. Swan said, "It is because he is so handsome."

"Then tell me," asked Little Lamb, "if your wife were to lose her beauty and your husband were to become ugly, would you still love each other?"

The swans smiled at each other and said, "Yes, we would still love each other very much."

"Then tell me again," asked Little Lamb, "why you love each other?"

Mr. Swan thought for a moment and said, "I know that if I need help my wife will be there to help me and that is why I love her." Mrs. Swan nodded her head to agree with her husband.

Little Lamb asked, "If your wife could not be there when you needed her, would you still love her?"

"Yes, I would love her even if she could not be there to help me." And Mrs. Swan smiled at her husband.

"Then tell me again," asked Little Lamb, "why do you love each other?'"

Mr. Swan thought again and said, "She will be a good mother for our children." And Mrs. Swan said, "He will be a good father for our children."

Little Lamb looked at his friends and asked, "What if you do not have any children, will you still love each other?"

The two swans looked at each other and said together, "Yes, we would still love each other very much. But tell us Little Lamb, if we loved each other even though we were ugly, or could not help each other, or could not have children, then why would we love each other so much?"

"You do not love ***because*** of any reason. Love is a precious gift given by God to all His children. When we feel God's love in us and around us we can give that love to all our brothers and sisters. You have decided to feel and enjoy God's love together. Enjoy God's gift of love. Sharing is the nicest part of any present."

And as Little Lamb waved goodbye the two swans swam off happily. In his heart Little Lamb could hear God's Voice, "As long as My children remember the love which I give to each of them, then they shall always have love to give and share with each other.

JUDGEMENT

Lion was waiting for Little Lamb as he walked through the mist into the dream.

"Little Lamb," cried Lion, "You must help me."

"How can I help you?" asked Little Lamb.

Lion looked sadly at Little Lamb and said, "All the animals come to me with their problems.

They want me to decide who is right and who is wrong. They want me to punish the wrongdoer, but I am not sure I am doing the right thing."

"Tell me about it," said Little Lamb.

And so Lion told him about two baby possums.

"They are always arguing," said Lion. "Their mother asked me to decide what to do."

Little Lamb smiled at Lion and said, "We can never make decisions by ourselves. We can only ask our Father to help us find an answer. For in His goodness and mercy He will send the answer to every problem."

Little Lamb and Lion closed their eyes and listened for their Father's answer. In their hearts they heard these words.

"Listen carefully My children. justice is being fair. Only through love can everyone gain and no one lose. Leave all judgment to Me, for I love my children and loving completely and equally is the only judgment there can be."

And so Little Lamb and Lion went to where the animals were waiting for them. Mother Possum was crying quietly. The baby possums waited near her.

Lion sat down on his rock and began, "You are here to ask my judgment on your problem. Both of you baby possums continue to fight and argue. Your mother is unhappy and you are unhappy. Let us solve this problem by asking our Father what to do."

And so they all closed their eyes and asked their Father for help. Each one of them heard an answer in his heart.

Lion looked up and said, "My answer is to leave all judgment to our Father for His judgment is to love everyone equally. All must gain and none must lose. Punishment makes losers. Love creates winners."

Mother Possum looked up and said, "my answer is to love both of my children equally and trust in their love for each other. For through their own love they will decide what to do."

As the baby possums smiled at one another the large possum said, My answer is to stop and ask our Father what to do whenever we start fighting."

The smaller possum then said, "And when we listen to God's answer He always shows us His love and then we want to share that love with each other. Who could stay angry when he is sharing love?" The two possums smiled at each other again.

Lion looked kindly at the possums and said, "We have asked our Father for help. And his judgment is to love equally and to trust in the sharing of that love. Go now and play. We have all learned our lessons well today."

As the possum family ran off into the forest, Little Lamb and Lion sat together happily. In their hearts they could feel God's love and wisdom, the only true judgment.

THE MIRACLE

"Little Lamb," called God.

"Yes, Father," answered Little Lamb.

"One of your brothers is dreaming and needs your help. In the dream he has forgotten his perfection which I gave him. Sleep, Little Lamb, and dream. Go into the dream and help your brother."

And in the dream Little Lamb opened his eyes. Long shadows covered the forest floor. Little Lamb could hear someone crying.

"Oh! Oh! My leg is broken. It hurts so much." Lying on the mossy ground was a spotted deer. Her eyes were closed with pain and her back leg was bent oddly.

Little Lamb walked over to the deer quickly. Scurrying around her was a little mouse. "Oh my, oh my," Mouse kept saying. "Miss Deer is much too big for a little mouse like me to move. Oh my, how can I help her?"

Owl sat on a branch overhead moaning, "No one can help her now. It is the end for her. If she can't run she will never be able to protect herself or find food to eat. No one can help her now."

And with that the deer cried more loudly for she was frightened and in pain.

Little Lamb looked down at the deer and smiled gently. "I know Who can help you Miss Deer. If you will but listen and believe, your leg will be healed."

The deer looked up with hope in her eyes. "I will listen Little Lamb. I want to believe."

"Gather 'round, Mouse and Owl," called Little Lamb. "Your sister needs all our help. Together with our Father we will heal her leg."

Mouse and Owl slowly came forward and sat next to Miss Deer. They all sat very quietly as Little Lamb spoke.

"God our Father is love. He can only create loving things and He created you. God our Father is perfect. He can create only perfect things and He created you. Do you believe that our Father is perfect and loving and creates only perfect and loving things?" asked Little Lamb.

Mouse felt God's kiss in the warmth of the sun and said, "Yes, I believe."

Owl listened to God's song in the sound of the buzzing insects and said, "Yes, I believe."

Miss Deer looked at the other animals and saw them each glowing with God's love and said, "Yes, I do believe."

As they all sat feeling each other's love and perfection the mist of the dream began to clear and they could see where they really were. Here was God's perfect world. They had never left it. And for a holy instant Little

Lamb, Miss Deer, Mouse and Owl were awake again in the peace and perfection of their Father's world.

But an instant doesn't last and when they looked again they were back in the dream. But something wonderful had happened.

"Look! Look!"' exclaimed Miss Deer. "My leg is healed. It doesn't hurt any more. I can even walk on it." And as the other animals watched, Miss Deer rose up on her legs and began to dance about merrily.

"It's a miracle," said Mouse.

"How is this possible?" asked Owl.

Little Lamb smiled. "Truly, through God's love anything is possible. We saw ourselves loving and perfect as our Father made us. And so God gave us the gift of a miracle, so we may remember His love and our perfection."

The breeze gently ruffled Little Lamb's wool. As Little Lamb opened his eyes he saw that he was awake and in his Father's world once more.

"You have done well today, My Son, " said his Father's Voice within his heart. "Today, for a holy instant, your brothers awoke from their dream and felt the love which I always have for them, and through that love was the gift of a miracle given."

THROUGH THE MIST

"Little Lamb, Little Lamb. Help me. I am alone and frightened. Little Lamb, please help me."

Little Lamb heard the call for help and drifted into the dream. He would come and he would help his brother in need.

Raccoon huddled close to the ground. His little body shook and shook with fear. All around him swirled a dark mist. All around him were dark angry looking clouds.

Little Lamb appeared at Raccoon's side. "I am so alone and afraid," Raccoon told Little Lamb.

"What are you afraid of?" asked Little Lamb.

"Don't you see? All around are dark clouds. All around the mist is so dark I cannot see through it. When I look closely at the mist I see things," said Raccoon shaking more and more as he looked around him.

"What things do you think you see in the mist?" asked Little Lamb.

"I see all the things I am afraid of. When I look in the mist I see myself getting hurt. I see myself alone with no one to love me. I am so afraid. What shall I do?" And Raccoon looked up at Little Lamb and his eyes filled with fear and unhappiness.

Little Lamb's heart went out to his friend. He knew just what he must do to help Raccoon.

"Do you have faith in my love for you?" Little Lamb asked Raccoon.

"Yes I do," said Raccoon.

"Do you want to leave these misty nightmares behind you and walk into the light?" asked Little Lamb.

"Yes, I do," said Raccoon hopefully.

"Then walk with me but a little way. Walk with me through the mists of the dream for that is what you see. Your nightmares are not real. They are only reflections of your fears in the mist around you. Just as a mirror will reflect your frowning face, so also will the mists around you reflect your fearful thoughts. Follow me and see how unreal your fears are." And Little Lamb began to walk forward through the dark clouds.

Raccoon wanted to believe Little Lamb for he knew Little Lamb loved him. And so he gathered up his courage and followed Little Lamb into the dark clouds.

As they walked side by side the mist began to part. All the frightening nightmares Raccoon saw in the mist began to disappear.

"Look!" cried Raccoon. And through the mist Raccoon could see the shining light. The closer they came to the light, the less mist there was until soon they walked together into the bright, loving light. All the mist was gone and all the frightening nightmares with it.

Raccoon looked up into the shining light. God's warm love surrounded him. Fear was gone and only happiness and peace remained in his heart.

Raccoon looked at Little Lamb and said with surprise, "My nightmares weren't real were they? As soon as I saw the light and followed it the mist began to disappear. Now I can see where I really am. I am in God's world and I was here all the time. I just didn't see it."

Little Lamb smiled, "Yes Raccoon. Just as the warmth of the sun makes the morning mist disappear, so too will the warmth of God's love make your misty nightmares disappear."

As Little Lamb and Raccoon stood together surrounded by the light of God's love they could hear God's Voice in them and around them saying," Welcome. I have been waiting for you to awake. Come and be at peace in the real world of love and happiness."

LIFE FOREVER

"Little Lamb, called God. "Your work is almost finished. Go into the dream world again. Your brothers need to know that life lasts forever.

As Little Lamb entered the dream he could hear Miss Deer talking loudly. "But it was a miracle. For a holy instant Little Lamb, the other animals and I were in God's real world and my broken leg was healed."

"I don't believe it," yelled Antelope, his antlers quivering with anger. "It was all a trick. Miracles can't really happen and this is the only world there is!" And with that Antelope turned to Little Lamb. "It is all your fault for giving these wild ideas to the animals."

In his anger Antelope lowered his antlers and butted Little Lamb, pushing him down to the ground. As Little Lamb fell his head hit a large stone and he lay very still.

For a moment there was frightened silence. Then Miss Deer began to cry. "Little Lamb is dead. Little Lamb is dead." And she began to cry more loudly.

All the other animals began to gather around, some of them crying, but all of them frightened.

Through the mist of the dream Little Lamb watched his friends standing and crying around his body. Little Lamb spoke to God his Father without words, "What shall I do now Father? All my brothers are sad and frightened because I have left my body. They think that I have died and am alive no more."

God spoke to Little Lamb," Go back into the dream Little Lamb. Show them that the body is just part of the dream. Show them that they use the body for learning. Show them that I have truly made them perfect and that there is no death, only beautiful life."

"My brothers," called Little Lamb to his friends in their hearts. "There is no death, for I am still alive."

Miss Deer looked around and said hopefully, "But where are you Little Lamb? I can hear your voice in my heart but I cannot see you. Your body is so quiet."

And as the other animals also heard Little Lamb within their hearts and listened, Little Lamb said, "I am here with you always, even as our Father is always with you. I am in the air you breathe, the water you drink, the clouds you look at and the grass you stand on. I am in your hearts, for this is where God's real world is. And here there is life forever."

As the animals watched, Little Lamb's body began to move slightly. His eyes began to flicker and his chest moved with deep breaths. Antelope exclaimed, "He lives! Little Lamb lives! He has come back to life."

Little Lamb stood up slowly and smiled at all his friends. As he looked around he could see Miss Deer smiling with happiness and love. Antelope's eyes were large with wonder and delight. And all the animals were quiet and filled with happy surprise.

"Truly," said Antelope. "Miracles do happen for I can see now that God's world is always around us."

"Yes," said Miss Deer. "And in God's world we are all perfect."

Little Lamb smiled at his friends and said, "Yes, our Father's world is filled with love and beauty. And in His world there could never be death, only beautiful life which lasts forever."

As the animals stood watching Little Lamb, a large beam of light fell on Little Lamb and he seemed to glow. And in their hearts all the animals could hear God's Voice saying, "This is your brother in whom I am well pleased. Today you are in My real world together. Come and enjoy the beauty and love I give to all of you. For I love each and every one of My children and give you all the gift of life forever."

AND WHO SHALL SAVE US?

All the animals of the forest were waiting for Little Lamb. In the center of the circle was a large stone for Little Lamb to sit on. And on the stone was a crown made of white daisies. The animals were quiet as they waited for Little Lamb to appear. He entered the dream and saw his brothers waiting for him.

Fat Robin came forward and met Little Lamb. She said, "Come sit on the stone in the center of the circle. This will be your throne. And here is a crown of daisies to place on your head."

Little Lamb looked at his friends and asked, "Why have you made a throne and crown for me?"

Fat Robin answered, "We want you to be our king. We want you to lead us and make our decisions for us. For you are wise and loving."

Then Miss Deer spoke up, "You have the power to perform miracles."

And Bear said, "You speak with God. You are His Son. Therefore we want to worship you."

Little Lamb looked around him sadly. "My brothers," he said, "I speak with God and when I listen to His Word I am wise and loving. But you cannot worship me. For though I am God's Son, so are you also."

"We are all the Sons of God and He has given His love and power and wisdom to all His children. I cannot make your decisions for you. You must listen for God's Voice yourself. I am powerful and wise because I listen to God's Voice, and He tells me what to do."

"But Little Lamb," called Miss Deer, "You perform miracles."

Gently Little Lamb said, "No, Miss Deer. I do not perform miracles. Miracles are a gift from God because we remembered His love for us and the perfection He gave us."

Then Antelope spoke up, "You were dead and you came to life again. Surely that is something special only you can do?"

Little Lamb smiled at Antelope and said, "God does not die, for God lives forever. I am God's Son, just as you are. I live forever and so do you."

"Then who shall lead us back to God? Who shall take us to heaven? Who shall save us?" asked all the animals.

As they sat quietly waiting for the answer, God's Voice spoke to each and everyone of them in his heart.

"My children, you are all saviors of the world. You are all My children and together, ***only*** together, shall My love be shared and completed. When you see My love in each of your brothers, then you shall know Me. When you give My love to each of your brothers then you shall know heaven. Who can save you? Why you can. For together with your brothers you shall save the world."

Miss Deer looked at Fat Robin and Antelope and said, "You are my brothers, and we are all God's children. Where His children are, so is He. Now I know where heaven is. It is right here, right now!"

And the animals looked at each other with love and understanding. God was with His children and they were in heaven with Him.

TOGETHER AT LAST

God spoke to Little Lamb in his heart, "All your brothers and sisters are ready to come home now. Go into the last dream and lead my children home." As Little Lamb walked through the mist of the dream he could see all the animals of the forest waiting for him.

The sun shone gently on each brother and sister making them glow with their Father's love. They smiled at Little Lamb and each other. And Little Lamb could feel God's gift of love in them and around them.

Little Lamb looked at all his brothers and sisters and said, "You have all learned your lessons here in the dream. The time for sleeping and dreaming is over. Let us all awake and go into our Father's world together." Little Lamb turned to Gray Squirrel, Bear and Large Goose, "What lesson did you learn so that you may awake into the real world?"

And the three animals smiled and answered together, "We must only ask for the answers to our problems and then listen for our Father's loving Voice. For in our Father's love is the answer to all our questions."

Little Lamb smiled and said, "Come with me into our Father's world."

Next Little Lamb looked at the two chipmunks and asked, What lesson did you learn so that you may awake into the real world?"

The chipmunks said, "We forgave each other. Anger comes from fear and fear disappears when love is shared."

Little Lamb smiled and said, "Come with me into our Father's world."

The Beaver stood up next as a clear, bright beam of light fell on his head, and he said, "My lesson was to choose happiness. God gives me only love and goodness. It was up to me to decide if I wanted to see that love and goodness."

"Then come with me into our Father's world," said Little Lamb.

Miss Deer, followed by Mouse and Owl, stepped forward and said, "Together we left this dream for a holy instant and saw God's real world. Through the gift of God's love a miracle was given to me and my broken leg was healed. It is time for us to return to our Father's world forever."

Little Lamb smiled and said, "Then come with me."

As Little Lamb looked around at the other animals the two swans spoke up, "Our lesson is to share God's love together." And they smiled lovingly at each other.

Gray Squirrel, Fat Robin and Pack Rat all said together, "Happiness is inside you. When you feel God's gift of love you feel happy and want to share it with everyone."

Little Lamb smiled and said, "You have learned your lessons well. Come with me into our Father's real world."

Lion spoke up next, "Justice is being completely fair, and only love can make everyone win and no one lose." Lion and all the animals felt God's judgment in their hearts. They were all brothers and sisters and could feel their Father's love equally.

Antelope walked forward quietly and slowly looked around. "Yes, let us all go home to our Father, for in the dream we see nightmares filled with death. We see anger and fear in our brothers and we feel anger and fear in our hearts. But in God's real world there is only love, peace, forgiveness, perfection and beautiful life forever."

Through the mist into the dream appeared Raccoon. "Hello friends. I have come back into the dream once more to help Little Lamb bring you home. Once before he helped me go through the mist and I learned my lesson: All the scary things I thought I saw in the dream were just reflections of my own fears."

Little Lamb smiled at all his friends and said, "The time has come. Let us walk but a little way together." And so they did. Through the mist they walked toward the bright light of their Father's love. As they walked the mist began to disappear and bright, loving light surrounded them. In their hearts they could all hear their Father's Voice. "Welcome home. The time for sleep and nightmares is over. Now is the time to awaken and see My real world. For I have created it with love as a most precious gift for My children. Come and enjoy what has always been yours."

And into their Father's world the animals came, filled with happiness, love and perfection.

PART II

The Children's Workbook

"Bring the little children to Me for in their innocence love is born."

INTRODUCTION

These meditations are sent to each of you so you may bring the truth home again to the little souls with whom you are working. Whether you are parent or teacher, your role is one of love and forgiveness. As you meditate with your charge you will experience the awareness of God through each other. Each meditation should be practiced at the end of the lesson; or at home in the morning and evening. This should be a time of quiet, warmth and tenderness, a most profound moment together; and together will you reach God.

Each lesson will be completed with a quiet period. This will allow students and teacher to meld together in the silence of God's love. This will be the time for the children's meditation. Children frequently develop talents and abilities in adapting to meditation, but most will not be able to sit quietly for long. Here is the secret to children's meditation: short, understandable and loving. The message will be loud and clear to each little soul listening with his heart. Be not disturbed if the children's reactions are not what you expect. Each child's body reacts differently to stimulation, including the spiritual kind. Bring patience, love and forgiveness with you to the meditation. Allow each child to express himself individually, without judgment.

Your group meditation should take place at the end of your lesson. Now is a quiet time for them to spend with you. They need not close their eyes, though it may help. The message of love will still make its way through the layers of ego to the heart of each little soul.

Read the meditation slowly and clearly. Then repeat the key phrases together. Ask the children to remember this idea all week, or until your next lesson. Now your tasks are finished for the day. Send your little ones home. Your lesson has been learned at the same time the little ones learned theirs.

LESSON 1

"God is love.
God can only create loving things,
And God created you."

Think for a moment about who you are and from where you come. Look at your father and then look at yourself. Does your father have hands and feet? So do you. Does your father have arms and legs? So do you. Can your father smile and laugh? So can you. Are you like your father? Yes, you are.

Now think about God, the Father of everyone and everything. God our Father is filled with love. He is love. You cannot see love. You can only ***feel*** love. Are you like your Father? Yes, you are. Feel your Father's love. For you are truly your Father's Son, and as He is filled with love, so are you also.

(Now read aloud together)

"God is love.
God can only create loving things,
And God created me."

LESSON 2

"God gives only kindness and love,
And God gives you everything."

How do you show love? You show love by doing loving things. How does God your Father, who loves you, show His love? He gives you kindness, happiness, peace and joy.

(Now read aloud together)

"God gives only kindness and love,
And God gives me everything."

LESSON 3

"Within my head God talks;
Within my heart God walks."

Where is God our Father? Don't look far, for He is inside you. He is that bright light of love which makes you what you are. He is the center of you. Now listen quietly for His Voice to help you. He is always inside you and He shall speak to you if you would just listen with your heart. Isn't it nice to know you are never alone?

(Now read aloud together)

"Within my head God talks;
Within my heart God walks."

LESSON 4

"Happy or sad,
Loving or scared;
Who decides? You do."

Look around you. Is the world bright and beautiful? Or is it dark and ugly? Do you see friends or do you see enemies? Do you feel happy and peaceful, or do you feel lonely and frightened? The room you see is only a room. You decide if it's ugly or beautiful. The people you see each day are all your brothers. You decide if they are your friends or enemies.

If you feel lonely and frightened then that is what you have decided to be. Now let's decide to be happy and peaceful. You are God's child. You can be anything you want to be.

(Now read aloud together)

"Happy or sad,
Loving or scared;
Who decides? I do."

LESSON 5

"Happy or sad,
Loving or scared;
Who helps you decide to be glad?
God does."

If we decide to be happy and decide to be frightened, then why would anyone stay frightened and unhappy? We could just decide to be happy. But we can't do it alone. We are part of God our Father Who is in us, and we must ask Him to help us decide to be happy. Together with God we can do anything; we can be anything. When we are together with God we are always happy.

The only decision we should make is to remember God is with us always and then we will always be happy.

(Now read aloud together)

"Happy or sad,
Loving or scared;
Who helps me decide to be glad?
God does."

LESSON 6

"What makes a shadow scary or friendly?
Your mind does."

Your mind tells you what to think. Your mind tells you whether you like what you see or whether you don't like what you see.

Your eyes see shadows all around you. Your mind decides if they are scary or friendly, for you cannot touch a shadow and a shadow cannot touch you. Shadows aren't real. It is only what you decide to think about them that makes them seem real.

When something or someone frightens you, remember you are only seeing shadows. Look for the light of God's love and it will shine away all the scary shadows that are not real.

(Now read aloud together)

"What makes a shadow scary or friendly?
My mind does."

LESSON 7

"What makes your best friend a friend when you play but an enemy when you fight? Your mind does."

We are all brothers. We have the same Father. He is loving and understanding; therefore we are loving and understanding. Your brother and you are the same. But you can decide to see him differently. You can decide not to like him. You can decide to fight with him. Or you can decide to love him, decide to understand him and decide to be happy together. Why would you want to fight and be unhappy? Your brother is just like you. He is loving and understanding, and so are you.

(Now read aloud together)

"What makes my best friend a friend when we play but an enemy when we fight? My mind does."

LESSON 8

"Be a perfect mirror. Reflect God's love."

Shine brightly. Polish away all the thoughts of hate and anger. Polish the mirror of your heart. For just like a mirror you will reflect what is in your heart. Polish away the dirt and grime and brightly reflect God's love. His love is like a light shining brightly. Let it shine on your heart and reflect love, growing brighter with each loving thought and deed.

(Now read aloud together)

"I am a perfect mirror. Let me reflect God's love."

LESSON 9

"Peace and love bring happiness
And joy your whole life through.
Peace and love bring happiness
Because God lives in you."

Whenever you are lost and afraid, whenever things are not going your way, remember this little prayer. God your Father is always there, and where He is, there you will find peace, joy and happiness.

(Now read aloud together)

"Peace and love bring happiness
And joy your whole life through.
Peace and love bring happiness
Because God lives in you."

LESSON 10

"Where is God?
Where is He not?
You need not look far
For God is here, there and everywhere."

Listen quietly and you will hear your Father speak to you. Look carefully with loving eyes and you shall see where your Father lives. He is not far away, for He would never leave His children alone. He is where you can always find Him. He is right here, right now!

(Now read aloud together)

"Where is God?
Where is He not?
You need not look far
For God is here, there and everywhere."

LESSON 11

"When God speaks the world listens;
His call of love breathes life to all."

Listen for your Father's Voice. It will speak to you through the sparrow's song; through the warm summer breeze; through the happy laughter of children. His Voice speaks to you of love and life. For without love there is no life. Listen for your Father's Voice; It is within your heart, and there is love.

(Now read aloud together)

"When God speaks the world listens;
His call of love breathes life to all."

LESSON 12

"Within our hearts God patiently waits;
Within God's heart we live and love."

God know's His children. God understands His Sons. God is always within you waiting patiently for you to listen to His loving Voice. Would a loving father leave his child alone and frightened? Feel God within you and know that He is in you and you are in Him.

(Now read aloud together)

"Within our hearts God patiently waits;
Within God's heart we live and love."

LESSON 13

"The wind—His gentle caress
The sun—His tender kiss
The rain—His tears of joy, cleansing and refreshing
The birds, insects and animals—Singing His songs of life
And all of this—His gift to His beloved children."

Thank you Father for Your love which you give to me, Your child.

(Now read aloud together)

"The wind—His gentle caress
The sun—His tender kiss
The rain—His tears of joy, cleansing and refreshing
The birds, insects and animals—Singing His songs of life
And all of this—His gift to His beloved children."

LESSON 14

"Speak only of love
And only God's Voice will be heard."

Tell the world about God's love and you become a tool for God's work. Hear His Voice telling you what to do and then let His words be yours when you speak. He knows what is good and right. He knows what is loving. Listen to Him and speak only what you hear in your heart. Look how easy it is. And see how happy it makes you.

(Now read aloud together)

"I will speak only of love
And only God's Voice will be heard."

LESSON 15

"Feel only God's peace
And heaven will surround you."

God is always here to guide and protect you. He will keep you safe and happy. All you need do is listen for His loving Voice and feel His loving touch within you and around you. Where is heaven, but in your hearts. You need not look far. For where God is, so also is heaven.

(Now read aloud together)

"I feel only God's peace
And heaven surrounds me."

LESSON 16

"I am one.
You are, too.
Behold the three: God the Father, you and me.
Together we make love's trinity."

Behold the Three: God the Father you and me. This is what love is all about. You are part of God; you are His child. Your brother is part of God; he is God's child also. If you are to love God, you must love all that is a part of God. And so we must love our brothers. God loves everything that is His. And we are His Children Whom He loves. Behold the Three; God the Father you and me. Together we make love's trinity. Together we are one.

(Now read aloud together)

"I am one.
You are, too.
Behold the three: God the Father, you and me.
Together we make love's trinity."

LESSON 17

"Make each day your very best;
Make each minute one of peace and rest;
Make each second a moment with God;
It's the path to joy; it's a happy heart."

You have two choices today. You can remember God is with you now, or you can forget He is here. If you choose to forget He is with you, you will feel lost, alone and frightened. But if you remember He is never away from you, always loving and always guiding and protecting, then you shall be happy and safe.

(Now read aloud together)

"Make each day your very best;
Make each minute one of peace and rest;
Make each second a moment with God;
It's the path to joy; it's a happy heart."

LESSON 18

"Each one of us is like each other...
Part of a whole; each part a brother."

Where do you end and your brothers begin? Where does God end and where does He begin? You may look different. You may look like you are separated from your brothers, but you are not just your body. You are much, much more. You are spirit. You cannot see or touch spirit. You can only feel spirit with your heart. This is where God is. This is what God is. He is spirit and so are you. Together with God and your brothers you are one. You are parts of the Whole and together you complete God's love.

"Each one of us is like each other...
Part of a whole; each part a brother."

LESSON 19

"Whenever you feel all alone
Just look and see Who's with you;
With every breath that you breathe in
Feel God's touch, He's in you."

He is your helper. He is your friend. He is the one who helps you all the time whenever you ask. He loves you and He is always with you. Breathe deeply and feel His love filling you. You are His Son whom He loves.

(Now read aloud together)

"Whenever I feel all alone
I just look and see Who's with me;
With every breath that I breathe in
I feel God's touch, He's in me."

LESSON 20

"A smile, a look, a helpful word...
Prayers of love from brother to brother."

What's the nicest way of saying I love you? It may be just a smiling face to give to someone sad. It may be just a look of love when someone feels they're bad. It may be just a word or two to help someone who's feeling blue. It doesn't matter what it is as long as love is sent from you.

(Now read aloud together)

"A smile, a look, a helpful word...
Prayers of love I give to my brothers."

LESSON 21

"Whenever someone seems to say,
'I don't love you, go away.'
Look deep within, for love is there,
Hiding far below his fear.
Fear that you don't love him too,
But you do love Him, and he loves you.
So whenever someone seems to say:
'I don't love you, go away,'
Look deep within for love is here,
Shining bright, forever near."

Don't be fooled by someone's angry face and words. Listen very carefully. For what they are really saying is that they are afraid and feel unloved. Their anger is a call for help and love. Let us help all our brothers. All we need to do is love them. Who could stay angry when love surrounds him?

(Now read aloud together)

"Whenever someone seems to say,
'I don't love you, go away.'
Look deep within, for love is there,
Hiding far below his fear.
Fear that you don't love him too,
But you do love Him, and he loves you.
So whenever someone seems to say:
'I don't love you, go away,'
Look deep within for love is here,
Shining bright, forever near."

LESSON 22

"To know your heart,
Look into your brother's eyes."

Your brother is a mirror of yourself. What do you see there? Do you see anger, fear, sadness? Or do you see happiness, peace, joy? If you do not like what you see in your brother, then look within yourself and change it there. Your brother is just a mirror of yourself. Feel happy and loving, and you will see happiness and love reflected in your brother also.

(Now read aloud together)

"To know my heart,
I must look into my brother's eyes."

LESSON 23

"Hold the thought of hurt and pain
And there you're trapped and there remain.
But hold the thought of joy and health
And know God's peace, His love, His wealth."

You are a Son of God. You can be whatever you want to be. Choose happiness and you will be happy. Choose fear and anger and you will be unhappy. Choose sickness and pain and you will have those also. And all you need to do is ***think*** about it, and it will be yours. Which do you want? Happiness or unhappiness; love or fear; health or sickness? God wants you to be happy, loving and healthy. Let's think His thoughts.

(Now read aloud together)

"If I hold the thought of hurt and pain
I will be trapped and there will remain.
But now I hold the thought of joy and health
And I know God's peace, His love, His wealth."

LESSON 24

"All our minds are one—We touch.
We touch in thought,
We touch in love.
For love is thought expressed to all."

We are all God's Sons. We are all connected by love. And what is love but a thought. We think with our minds. And our minds are one. All we need do is think of love and we will be one with all our brothers and with God all at once. Isn't love wonderful?

(Now read aloud together)

"All our minds are one—We touch.
We touch in thought,
We touch in love.
For love is thought expressed to all."

LESSON 25

"Open up your eyes and heart
Like petals on a flower.
Open up your eyes and heart
To feel God's love and power."

Have you really looked around you lately? Have you really listened carefully? What do you see and hear? If you really look and listen you will hear God's Voice calling to you in the rustle of the leaves, or the roar of the freight train, or the happy laughter of your friends and family. He is always there. Just look closely and listen. You can hear Him now. He is saying "I love you."

(Now read aloud together)

"I open up my eyes and heart
Like petals on a flower.
I open up my eyes and heart
And feel God's love and power."

LESSON 26

"You're in God's Mind
So think His thoughts."

If God is love, then what kind of thoughts would God have? Why loving thoughts, of course. If you are God's Son, then you are love also. What kind of thoughts would you have? Why loving thoughts, of course. Listen to your Father's Voice and think His Thoughts with Him, for they are your thoughts also. They belong to you. Think love, for you are love.

(Now read aloud together)

"I'm in God's Mind
So I think His thoughts."

LESSON 27

"Where is God's world?
Right here, Right now.
Can you see God's world?
Yes, with loving eyes, that's how."

Heaven isn't far away. Heaven is right here. Every time you are filled with love and happiness you are remembering your real home. Every time you share love with your brothers you are giving a piece of heaven to someone else and heaven grows with the giving. Where is heaven? Right here. Right now.

(Now read aloud together)

"Where is God's world?
Right here. Right now.
Can I see God's world?
Yes, with loving eyes, that's how."

LESSON 28

"Be ever alert to God's own thoughts:
They are Thoughts of love.
They are Thoughts that heal.
They are Thoughts of oneness to know and to feel."

Listen carefully to the thoughts you think. You will always know when you are thinking God's Thoughts with Him. His Thoughts make you happy. His Thoughts make you well. His Thoughts are filled with love and joy. His Thoughts are yours. All you need do is think them.

(Now read aloud together)

"Be ever alert to God's own thoughts:
They are Thoughts of love.
They are Thoughts that heal.
They are Thoughts of oneness to know and to feel."

LESSON 29

"Pain and death
Or joy and life
The choice is yours."

Who decides what your body will be like? Is it strong? Is it healthy? Is it weak? Is it sick? What would God make your body like? Would He make you sick? Never. Would He make you weak? Never. Would He make you strong and healthy? Of course! He loves you. He gives you everything. But it is up to you if you want to accept His gifts. Which do you choose?

(Now read aloud together)

"Pain and death
Or joy and life.
The choice is mine."

LESSON 30

"God's gift to you is life."

Life is more than breathing in and out. Life is being happy. Life is feeling peace and joy. Life is knowing God is always with you. Life never ends. Life is for always. And it is always yours.

(Now read aloud together)

"God's gift to me is life."

LESSON 31

"Place your hands in God's
And He will lead you home."

Your Father's loving hands are always there to help you. In your heart you will hear His Voice, guiding you and showing you the way. And as you listen you will feel His hands taking yours and leading you to safety. God's home is your home. God's home is heaven and you have never left it.

(Now read aloud together)

"I place my hands in God's
And He will lead me home."

LESSON 32

"Heal yourself by asking God's help."

If God doesn't make you sick, then who does? You do. You choose sickness or pain or unhappiness. How can you become healthy and happy? By simply changing your mind. Can you do it alone. No, you can't. That is why God is always there to help you. All you have to do is ask.

(Now read aloud together)

"I heal myself by asking God's help."

LESSON 33

"Change your mind—And change the world.
Heal yourself—And the world is healed with you."

You are a part of God and God is a part of everything and everyone. You are in God and God is in everything and everyone. You are a Thought of God and God's Thoughts are everything and everyone. You are never alone and what you think and what you do affects everything for you are a part of God.

(Now read aloud together)

"I change my mind—And I change the world.
I heal myself—And the world is healed with me."

LESSON 34

"Your brother shares his thoughts with you.
Your thoughts are his; false or true.
True thoughts bring love,
False bring sorrow.
Which would you think?
Which would you follow?
Which would you give your brother as gifts?
Which would you want from
Your brother as presents?
Your brother shares his thoughts with you.
Your thoughts are his; false or trite
True thoughts bring love,
False bring sorrow."

Now let's say together: *"I give the gift of love to my brother."*

LESSON 35

"Sharing, helping, loving, feeling;
Thoughts of God; thoughts of healing."

God's Thoughts are always in your mind. But sometimes we forget them. All we must do is think of loving things we want to do for our brothers. All we need think about is happiness, joy, sharing and helping. These are God's Thoughts, and they are our thoughts too. Help yourself and help your brother today. How wonderful and how simple it is.

(Now read aloud together)

"By sharing, helping, loving, feeling,
I think God's Thoughts: I think of healing."

LESSON 36

"Take the time to love your brother."

Look at all the things your mind thinks about all day. Think about all the thoughts you have. How many of your thoughts are about your brothers? How many of your thoughts about your brothers are loving thoughts? Let's spend more time thinking loving thoughts about our brothers.

(Now read aloud together)

"I will take the time to love my brother."

LESSON 37

"Where will you find your Father?
He is looking out from behind your brother's eyes."

God our Father is not far away. God lives in you and He lives in me, and He lives inside your brother. All you need do to find your Father and your Father's love is to look closely at your brother. There is love and there is happiness. Look deep within your brother's eyes and know His home and yours and mine.

(Now read aloud together)

"Where will I find my Father?
He is looking out from behind my brother's eyes."

LESSON 38

"To find your Father
Look deep within your brother."

Do not ignore your brother's gift of love. It is your Father's gift of love given through your brother. There, in your brother is the home you have been looking for. There, in your brother's love will you find the love you are looking for. There is God; there is heaven; there is joy.

(Now read aloud together)

"To find my Father
I must look deep within my brother."

LESSON 39

"Happiness is shared by all."

See how catchy a smile is. See how catchy a laugh is. Giggle and smile and the world wants to join you. Now think about your smiling thoughts. They are catchy too. Send the world some giggles and a smile. You will feel good and the world will feel good with you.

(Now read aloud together)

"My happiness is shared by all."

LESSON 40

"Open your eyes and see your brother...
Shining bright, shining clear;
A mirror of your love,
A reflection of your Father."

Your brother is the mirror for your love. Let your love shine brightly so it may reflect off your brother and bless you with happiness. See your brother as loved and loving and you will be loved and loving also.

(Now read aloud together)

"I open my eyes and see my brother...
Shining bright, shining clear;
A mirror of my love,
A reflection of my Father."

LESSON 41

"Who speaks to you when you're alone?
Who guides you and directs you home?
God does."

Now you know who loves you best. Now you know where to find His love. Now you know how to hear your Father's loving Voice. Listen silently to His Voice, for it will show you the way home. It will show you happiness and joy. It is the Voice of Love."

(Now read aloud together)

"Who speaks to me when I'm alone?
Who guides me and directs me home?
God does."

LESSON 42

"Remember who and what you are;
Remember you are God's own Son."

God is spirit. And so are you. God is love. And so are you. God gives happiness and joy; and this you receive. God creates heaven; and that is your home. God is your Father, and you are His Son. What a wonderful family we have.

(Now read aloud together)

"I remember who and what I am;
I remember I am God's own Son, and I am happy."

LESSON 43

"Love bursts forth across your mind;
God's own love: It's yours...It's mine."

Feel the mighty power of love. It brings you all you ever need. It brings you love and happiness and peace. It connects you with all your brothers. It connects you with your Father. Love is like the mighty rope that ties us all together. Feel God's love and know it's yours forever.

(Now read aloud together)

"Love bursts forth across my mind;
God's own love: It's yours...It's mine."

LESSON 44

"Open up your heart and know;
God is here and heaven is now."

We look all over to find the things that will make us happy. Sometimes we think it will be a toy, but soon we tire of it. Sometimes we think it is a place to visit, but the fun we have only lasts a moment.

You do not have to look far to find happiness. Happiness is God, and God is always with you. Happiness is heaven, and the home of heaven is in God's love. Don't look far, for God is here and heaven is now.

(Now read aloud together)

"I open up my heart and know;
God is here and heaven is now."

LESSON 45

"Faith and trust, hope and love;
Prayers and gifts to God above."

God gives us everything. He gives us the most precious gift of all—His love. And His love will make us happy and peaceful. What does God ask in return? The only gift our Father wants is for us to have faith and trust in His love for us. How simple it is. All we need do is send love out from us and we will receive God's gift of love in return.

(Now read aloud together)

"Faith and trust, hope and love;
Prayers and gifts to God above."

LESSON 46

*"Place your faith in God your Father.
He leads you home, you and your brother."*

You cannot come home alone. Your brother must come with you. How can you and your brother go home together? That is easy. Just send your brother love. See him happy. See him healthy. See him perfect. See him as a Son of God, just like you. And then together will God your Father lead you home to heaven.

(Now read aloud together)

*"I place my faith in God my Father.
He leads me home, me and my brother."*

LESSON 47

*"Who guides us and directs us home?
Who knows our needs and joys?
Who gives us everything and more? God does."*

Let God lead you home. Let God make you happy. Let God give you everything you need. The only thing you must do is open your heart to His loving Word. And the Word is love. Listen for his message. In everything you think and do, listen for the love that is there. Send that love from you to your brothers and receive from God the blessings of heaven, now.

(Now read aloud together)

*"Who guides me and directs me home?
Who knows my needs and joys?
Who gives me everything and more? God does."*

LESSON 48

"We are God's Son.
We are love.
We are home, in heaven, now."

Are we our bodies? No, we are spirit. Are all our thoughts God's thoughts? No, only happy, loving thoughts are God's Thoughts. Who decides whether we will think happy or unhappy thoughts? We do. What are you really like? You are love, and love always brings joy. Where is your home? Your home is in heaven, and heaven is right here, right now. All you need do is feel loving and happy and you will find heaven, now.

(Now read aloud together)

"We are God's Son.
We are love.
We are home, in heaven, now."

LESSON 49

"I am as God created me."

Did you really listen to what I just said?
"I am as God created me."
Say this with me now:
"I am as God created me."

Think about what that means. God created only love. God gives only happiness and joy. God is your Father, and you are like your Father.
Say this with me again:
"I am as God created me."
"I am perfect."
"I am love."
"I am God's Son."
Now let us say again one more time:
"I am as God created me."

LESSON 50

"We go together to our Father's home."

Our lessons for the year are almost over. We have learned Who our Father really is. We have learned who we really are. We have learned it is our decision, not God's, to be happy or not. We know God only gives love. And we have learned the most important thing: "We cannot reach our Father's home unless we take our brothers with us. Show each of your brothers total love. Give him your happiness and joy, and together God will lead you home."

(Now read aloud together)

"We go together to our Father's home."

LESSON 51

"I am home."

Heaven is the home of happiness. Heaven is filled with peace and love. Heaven is deep within your heart. There is God our Father. There, if we will but listen, is the message, that will give us everything we could ever want. We have learned to listen and hear God's word of love. We have learned to send His love out to all our brothers. We have learned how to be in heaven right now. We simply must choose to be happy and loving. Where are you right now?

(Now read aloud together)

"I am home."

LESSON 52

"Come little children and you shall hear about your Father in heaven:"

"Where is heaven?" (Now let the children answer)

But in my heart.

"How can you find heaven?"

But I must look within.

"How shall you know heaven?"

But God my Father will speak to me.

"How shall you hear your Father?"

But by keeping all my thoughts still.

"And what message shall your Father send you?"

But that I am a part of Him and He is everything.

"When will you know your Father?"

But I never knew Him not!

Epilogue...

You and your student have followed a steep path on a long journey. Together you have stepped out of time by using time, and you have come closer to the awareness of your true reality.

Remember only the joy this past year has brought you. Look back only to see how far you have come and realize the journey you made was helped by One Who knows your needs and guided you along the path which you chose.

Now your work has just begun, for now you have begun to feel alive. Now you have begun to see your true role. Now you have begun to assume your true function. You are the savior of the world and together with your student you will be saved.

Begin your work now. For God is with you always and it is His will with yours which will guide you home.

PART III

Instructions
For Working With Children

INTRODUCTION

To all who would be teachers of young minds...

The tasks you are to perform will come down through the levels of awareness until the minds touch. Here you will seek salvation. Here you will seek oneness with those you help. Do not forget the reason for your function. The goal is understanding; the means will be love; the reward will be freedom.

Each child represents an aspect of yourself expressed uniquely. Each child answers the need to fulfill your function of forgiveness. Each child and teacher together fulfill the promise given by God to his Sons when the separation occurred. Now together you will complete the promise of oneness, the return to God.

The child's mind must be approached on two levels. First it must be gently opened to the thought patterns for which we are striving. This should be accomplished with extreme care and love, each petal gently unfolded as if by the loving kiss of the sun.

Each child, already formed spiritually, must be experienced uniquely. Through these experiences, you as teacher, will reverse roles and learn through the child's unquestioning faith in love. Some children already will have had the stamp of ego impressed firmly on their thought patterns, but even these will have the magnificent pliability to grow, expand and learn. On this second level you, the teacher, will learn.

Lessons can be planned through the material available to you. Each lesson will revolve around an important concept; but in all cases your own love and creativity, channeled through you from the Holy Spirit, should be the guiding factor.

Materials will become available to help you demonstrate concepts. But always remember that it will be the child himself who will supply the main ingredient in each lesson. Your job will be to listen, and by listening to the Holy Spirit within each child you will be witness to his growth.

Go forth and lead My children home. In their innocence love is born and through the loving expression of their lives My Word is sent forth. Fulfill your function with love and gratitude.

Your first lessons with any child will be to open his mind to the idea that heaven is within himself. He must begin to realize that the world around him will seem to change simply by his own change in attitude and perspective. The hell he thinks he lives, the nightmares experienced when awake or asleep, is his growing acceptance of ego and separation. He is learning to accept himself as a limited being, limited by his physical manifestation. Now will be the time for us to end his downward spiral into ego-orientation and reverse the cycle upward to the expansion of universal love.

The practical application of this will be to show him the way to look at things differently. For example: What makes a shadow friendly or scary? His mind does. As each child looks through his own experiences your job will be to help him see the holiness within them. Use stories, personal experiences and supplemental material to illustrate your points. Allow the brightness of your spirit to shine through the clouds around each child and to help him bask in the love of his Father.

The following lessons will cover the child's budding awareness of his illusory world. This is important. Allow him free expression during these periods. When enough time is spent on acknowledging illusions, then the next stage of learning will take place.

Now his lessons on forgiveness will come. Through these lessons the child will learn the process of overlooking sin. For what he believes to be sin is simply illusion which in reality never occurred. The bedrock of this course is to teach forgiveness. Now comes the challenge of awakening the child's awareness of his brother's needs, and through his acceptance of his forgiven brother he will forgive himself. These lessons will cover much time and should be handled delicately. Within these lessons gentle counseling will take place. Provide ample opportunity for the children to counsel each other. Here they will begin their own work with their brothers. Your job as teacher will be to mediate and to guide the children's counseling among themselves rather than to lecture. Within these lessons you will form the fundamental approach to miracles. This will be the heart of your work.

Children are constantly functioning on a receptive level. This will allow you to dip deeply into the wellspring of wisdom which is harbored in each child's heart. Material specifically prepared for the young mind will be presented to each of you. The concrete not the abstract must be the learning format.

Through the Rays of Light will knowledge be opened.

ADAPTATION

Learning—Teaching

Working with children is one way of expressing and living the Word. We are one and through our acknowledgment of oneness we will begin to learn Truth. It will be through the path which each one seeks that his knowledge will become manifest. The children will learn and teach. Their paths have directed them to you their teacher. But where is that dividing line between teacher and student? Their learning sequence is correlated closely with yours. Learn well the lessons your students teach you for it is through their inner wisdom expressed to you that your growth will be assured.

Learning involves a reawakening to truths already held deeply within the heart. Awakening to these truths is our sole purpose here on earth. When each and everyone can be aware of his ultimate destiny, heaven will be proclaimed on earth and illusions will disappear from awareness.

Teaching involves the demonstration of what you are learning. It is through this reinforcement of your own lessons that you become witness of God's world for others. Do not confuse the two, learning and teaching, as opposites. For it is only through the combination of both that reality can be shared. Do not deny your existence by denying the truth hidden within each of your students. Their reality is yours. Their love is a reflection of your own. Teach well, for it is through your efforts that you will learn.

Take the child's hand and lead him through the brambles of illusions to the inner path of truth. Together reality will unfold, for it is only through your brother that you may reach salvation. Now go in peace and learn your lessons through teaching.

Learn well the concept you think you are teaching the child, for it is this very same lesson which you must learn also. Do not assume that because you are the "teacher" you have learned the lessons. You would not be teaching them if this were so.

Watch each student who comes before you closely. He is an expression of yourself which you have not allowed yourself to recognize. This is his purpose for being there, just as your presence is an opportunity for him to see aspects of himself reflected in you. Through the eyes of love you will experience Christ. See Christ in each of your students and thereby find Christ in yourself.

Oneness of God

Let us consider the problem of bringing these concepts to the young mind. At an inner level all children, as well as adults, are fully aware of Truth. It is only in its upward travel from the subconscious to conscious that much is lost and distorted. Here, in the ego-oriented realm, we analyze and choose those facts which will reinforce what our five senses record.

The idea of oneness with our brothers is an abstraction difficult for an adult to understand, but not impossible for a child. Spiritual awareness must be triggered. This is your role. Body or ego-orientation must be minimized and spiritual oneness emphasized.

In the child's mind God becomes an all powerful parental figure separated from him. Because of our limitation to the five senses His power seems to transcend ourselves. This can be either comforting or frightening. Help free the child from his fears and place all emphasis on God's love which surrounds him, fills him and guides him. Remember always to express God's love as something within rather than without. Bring the awareness of God's presence into correct focus. He is within. Your Self is within and so you are with God, in God and of God. Bring the awareness of his holiness upward to consciousness within the child and free him from the imprisoning ideas of ego.

The Holy Spirit's Guidance

Let the Holy Spirit guide you in all your work and you will then be able to teach your students to do the same. By allowing the Holy Spirit to guide you, you will be witness to the presence of God within rather than without. Children need to know that there is something upon which they can depend. Their world, a magnified version of the adult world, is one of powerful adversaries. To this we must address our efforts. To the child, the whole world can be either a frightening enemy or adventurous friend. In either case his feelings of inadequacy are apparent. He seems to have little effect over his surroundings. The surroundings seem to affect him.

Reliance on the Holy Spirit's loving guidance must come next. Each child must be taught to look within himself and to listen for his Father's Voice within his heart. Here will be the answer to his problems and guidance for his decisions. The method will be teaching prayer and meditation. Individual and group meditation techniques must be taught. How peaceful the world would be if each adult and child spent just a few minutes with his Father unifying their spirits consciously.

Through individual prayer and with God's help the child will learn to find his own answers. Group meditation during your teaching periods will help solidify the unity of spirit so necessary to the concept of brotherhood. This is the heart of counseling: To pray together and hear God's Word simultaneously, the miracle occurring.

The Holy Spirit's function is the link between the inner self, or God awareness, with the outer self. Too often we forget to contact our innermost Self, the seat of heaven, the throne of God.

In teaching young minds to go within, it is necessary to help them discern the difference between ego-imaginings and true silence, the silent knowledge of truth. Teach them to release their awareness from daydreams of reality and come deep into full awareness of the real world. Peace, happiness, joy: These will be the guideposts for their journey within. Take the child gently to the door and help him knock. The Holy Spirit will help him open the door and walk within. Your job is to show him how to get there and how to ask. This will be accomplished through the simple prayers given at the end of each lesson. Discuss them; use them; allow the children a short quiet time to meditate on them. This will be the road to awareness. Thus time will be used to reach the Father.

Illusion

The child's mind is filled with fantasies. He lives in the active world of illusion building. You call them games. As adults you have forgotten you are still illusion building and still playing games. Games are of the ego. Spirituality of purpose is reality.

It is within the illusion that the child begins to see himself represented. The illusion becomes all his points of reference. He becomes a pawn of the illusion instead of its maker.

Your job as teacher will be to help the child out of this limited sphere and to help him to acknowledge his limitlessness. The first area to be approached will be thought. It will be through his awareness of the power of thought that he will gain conscious control over his environment. "The Choice"* will be an excellent starting place to begin discussion of what the mind can do. Here we have two points of view about one specific point of action. This idea can be expanded to include all of the child's experiences of the week or day. His friends can help him see the different ways of looking at his world. In this way all the children can widen their awareness of the power of thought and attitude. Now he begins to see how he forms his own happiness and unhappiness. His world brightens with the light of understanding. His consciousness begins to take direction from his Self through the Holy Spirit's guidance. He is now beginning to listen.

*(See the story "The Choice" in Little Lamb, Part I)

Thought

Now will be the time to introduce the all-encompassing aspects of thought: There are no private thoughts; there are no neutral thoughts. Each of these concepts must be approached separately and then brought together into the focus of forgiveness and the resultant miracle.

As the connected essence of Oneness we could no more think private thoughts than we could separate ourselves from our Father. We are spirit combined and indivisible, whole and holy, the Creation.

As we are part of God, so do we also have the power of God. He gives us the freedom, the glory and the power. We are the Thoughts of God and in His image are our thoughts powerful.

Choose your thoughts wisely: ego or spirit; fear or love; unhappiness or happiness. To which thought system do you wish to listen. These ideas and options must be presented to each child. He must become aware of the power of his thoughts and the necessity of listening to and choosing from the thought system which will bring him only happiness. Help him choose wisely for through your loving guidance will salvation be yours and his.

Now that he has become aware of his power he must also become aware of his responsibility.

Forgiveness

He must learn that only through forgiveness of his brother will he and his brother be saved. Show him that as he sees his brother's perfection he shall see his own. Help him to reflect God's love onto his brother so he may receive it in turn.

His brother's love is there for the asking. He must open his eyes to its presence and accept the gift already offered him, but within the illusion, veiled and unseen. His brother's love shines forth seeking recognition. Let us not deny him that gift of giving. These are the lessons which will take endless teaching. Through your own demonstration of forgiveness toward the children with whom you work, as well as your gentle guidance as they counsel each other, you and they will find God's presence.

Use prayer and meditation as well as allegorical stories. The children will relate to the animals and their problems. Through the animals the children can become observers of their own experiences. *

Through forgiveness the world is saved from its illusions of fear and guilt. The children with whom you are working need the assurance that their world is not filled with malice and hate, fear and revenge. Through the outward expression of their inner light and love they will see their reflection in their brother. Each child needs the reassurance that only through his constant giving, not taking will he receive. Here is that very different but oh so rewarding lesson, directly opposite to the ego's interpretation: To give IS to receive. Show each child that as he gives so shall he receive the same in return. As he shows love to his brothers so shall he receive love in return. Conversely, as he shows fear to his brother so shall that be returned also.

This is a very easy lesson for the children to help illustrate. There isn't one instance of interpersonal relationships the children have been through that day or week which cannot be used to explain this concept. The arguments and bickering which seem to escalate and spiral between children are easily used as illustrations. Remember to emphasize the children's basic and usually unquestioning generosity for it is through the positive examples that the concept of forgiveness will be reinforced.

*(See Little Lamb, Part I)

Sharing, Not Bargaining

In all special relationships there is an element of bargaining. You see another as the answer to a need. You agree to give that person "love" in the hopes of receiving something in return. When your desires are not specifically met, you retract your "love." Now you extend fear and anger hoping that by making the other guilty they will return your "gifts; " and so they do, returning fear and guilt in turn to you.

Now is the time to show children that they must not bargain, but share. In bargaining the only exchange between brothers is fear and guilt, a heavy burden to carry. Through the sharing of God's love, without questioning or looking for a specific outcome, shall joy be felt.

Love is a glorious gift given to each of us, for it is truly the essence of God Himself. To share with another is simply the acknowledgment of that love which shines radiant and pure within us. God's gift of love remains with you. The tragedy is your blindness to it. Help open the eyes of the children with whom you work by opening your own. As you see the perfection in each of your students so shall the brightness within them be reflected to you in greater magnitude, shining away the dark places in all your hearts.

Miracles

The basis for the awakening process is within the miracle. it is through this illusion, sent by the Holy Spirit and used for Holy purpose, that you and the children will be aware of God.

Teach well the dynamics of miracles.

1. Recognize that a healing must take place.
2. Ask the Holy Spirit's guidance.
3. Listen. This is so important, for what good is asking if you refuse to listen.
4. Faithfully trust in the Holy Spirit's sure guidance. The healing has taken place. Hold fast to that belief and allow the Holy Spirit to use you, time and place according to His wise judgment. Faith is a key word. It is only through your faith in the Holy Spirit and the sure knowledge that miracles are natural that they will become apparent to you.

Your work is beginning. You, the teachers of young minds, listen well. Listen to your Self. Listen to the Self in each of your students. Listen for the Holy Spirit's sure guidance within all that you see, hear and do.

Miracles are your right to be shared and experienced with all your brothers. Miracles heal. Let the Holy Spirit heal you and your brothers simultaneously and heaven shall be yours now.

You are ready to use these concepts with your students. They will come to you for now you are ready to learn from them.

APPLICATION

Sequence of the material presented should follow a very carefully formulated pattern. The child-mind must be introduced to the concepts in small easily digestible doses. Beginning with awareness of self, in conjunction with the universe, he can begin to assimilate information showing his relationship to others and the individual relationship to the whole or God.

Once his position in the universal consciousness is determined he can then develop an understanding of the way he affects the world he perceives and the way he is affected only by his thoughts. This is crucial to his growing understanding of miracles. In all lessons, over and over, the concept of leaving judgment to the Holy Spirit should be emphasized.

Now that his place in the universe has been established and the effects of thought given application, he will be able to apply these concepts to his everyday life. We now have a budding teacher of God. How exhilarating! To be able to help mold spiritual growth is truly the work of saints.

Now that the pattern has been formed you will be ready to begin day to day lesson plans. Each lesson will be followed by a short prayer period. This will be the opportunity to introduce the actual workbook lessons. Use these lessons as the basis for your prayer segment. Help the children reach deeply within themselves for the answers to their problems. Within the heart the seeds of love lie dormant waiting for the blessed water of enlightenment.

Suggested Lesson Plan

1. Short discussion of the past week. This allows the children to be comfortable with each other.
2. Story, play, songs, puppets, film. This will be the presentation of the day's concept.
3. Discussion. Allow the children to express any and all feelings about the presentation. Guide the children toward the basic truth given.
4. Counseling. Help the children help themselves and each other through the practical application of the concept presented.
5. Prayer. Use this time to teach meditation based on the workbook lesson. Some preliminary explanation may be necessary, but the concept for the day should coincide with the prayer.

Suggested Questions and Sequence

Each of these suggested questions can form the basis for your teaching format. Expand on these even further as you wish. Allow the flow of ideas to expand your lessons rather than restrict them. This is a course in illumination. Do not stifle your growth or your students'.

1. Teach the oneness of the Son with the Father
   Who are we?
   How do we see ourselves as limited?
   Why do we see ourselves as limited?
   What is spirit?
   Where does spirit live?
   Wholeness and the Sonship,

2. Reality vs. reality
   What is real?
   What things change?
   How does thought affect how we see life?
   How does thought affect our bodies?
   Does love change?

3. Relinquishment of ties to ego
   Begin counseling among students.
   Open their thoughts to love, away from fear.
   Listen for the Holy Spirit's instructions.
   Give up judgment.

4. Special Relationship to Holy Relationship
   Forgiveness. This should be stressed repeatedly.
   Counseling among students.
   Is love or fear expressed in a relationship?
   How to shift from fear to love.

5. Oneness of the Sonship
   Review and expand the concept of spirit.
   How is brotherhood shown?
   Can separation truly be a reality?

6. What are miracles?
   When do miracles occur?
   The natural quality of miracles.
   The dynamics of miracles.

PART IV

Help Is On The Way

A Miracles Course for Slightly Older Children

Chapter I

Jerry trudged up the street. Each footstep bringing him closer to impending disaster. Under his arm was a stack of school books. Slipped between the pages of his math book were his orders for execution -- his report card from school. It wasn't so much the punishment that would be a week of no television or the withholding of his allowance which caused him despair. No, it wouldn't be the punishment. As he looked up at his house, painted gray and black and looking even more gray through the blackness of his fear, he knew the worst would be the faces on his mother and father.

Quickly he climbed the front steps, slipping quietly into the front hallway. He placed his books on the table by the front door, his report card on top. He knew it was just a matter of time before he would have to show it to his mother, but later seemed to much better than right now.

"Jerry? Is that you?" called his mother from the kitchen. He could hear the water running in the kitchen sink and he knew she was preparing supper. There was no getting away from it now. Jerry could hear the executioner's footsteps in his head. The time was getting near.

"Yes, Mom. It's me." Jerry listened carefully to what his mother was saying. The way she said things usually told him what kind of a mood she was in. She sounded pretty calm. That was good. Now the question was what kind of mood would his father be in when he returned home from work.

"Why don't you run up and get washed, Jerry," said his mother. "Oh, by the way did you get your report card in school today?"

Jerry stood quietly as he nibbled on a piece of carrot. His mother turned toward him. He didn't have to say a word. She always knew what was on his mind. "So it was that bad," she said, her face tightening. "You had better go wash, and we will talk about it after dinner. "

Jerry swallowed hard several times. It seemed his throat and stomach were in knots. He turned and headed upstairs to his room. At least there he could be among the things that made him happy. Hanging from the ceiling were the airplane models he had proudly finished last month. On his dresser were the trophies from Little League and wrestling. But peace and quiet were not to be his yet. Opening the door with a slam and a shriek was his sister Angie. "Jerry! Jerry my kite string is all tangled up. Look at the knots. Help me get them out please?" The last sentence ended with a whine. Jerry hated his sister to whine.

"Why should I help you with your crummy kite? You always mess things up, so it's up to you to unmess them. And besides, who told you to come in my room without asking permission, huh?"

All of Jerry's worry and anger came out at his sister. Her face contorted into frustration and she burst into tears. “It’s not a crummy kite. It’s a beautiful kite. I can’t help it if the string gets knots.”

“Why can’t you two be with each other for two seconds without fighting?” Their mother stood in the doorway with her hands on her hips, her voice raised in anger. Jerry’s heart sank lower as he realized any good mood she might have been in before, was gone now. Sure enough the next remark was directed toward him. “I would think you were in enough trouble already, young man, instead of getting into more. We have a lot to talk about with your father tonight, don’t we?” And with that his mother left the room dragging his sister with her.

“Boy, now I’m really in for it,” thought Jerry. Anger, frustration, and guilt welled up within him. He balled his fist and hit the wall next to him. As the pain shot up his arm he thought, “I’m always making a mess. My life is just like those knots in Angie’s kite string. All knotted and messy and no way for me to get them out. “ He rolled over on his bed and waited for supper, though he knew he wasn’t going to be able to eat very much.

SOME THINGS TO THINK ABOUT

1. How do you feel when you bring home your report card?

2. Do you have brothers and sister? How do you get along with them?

3. How do your parents treat you when you argue with your brothers and sisters?

Chapter 2

Jerry's room was almost dark, the furniture fading into the walls, when he heard his father open the front door. Jerry waited until he could hear the rattle of the pots and pans against the dishes as his mother served dinner. "Jerry! Angie! It's time for supper," called his mother. Slowly Jerry got up front his bed and went downstairs.

Angie was already at the table with his father, while his mother filled glasses with milk. Jerry's father was a tall man with dark, thinning hair. His large hands were folding his napkin over his knee as he looked up at Jerry with deep-set gray eyes. The same eyes looked back at him from Jerry's face. Although Jerry had his mother's light colored hair, the rest of his features were his father's. And as he grew older and taller the resemblance was becoming more pronounced. "Hi, Jer." His father called. "How's it going?" Obviously Jerry's mother hadn't told his father about the report card or the fight with Angie. Cautiously Jerry replied, "Oh, just fine I guess." He slipped into his seat hoping the rest of the meal would go as smoothly.

For the most of the meal the family ate quickly and silently. Occasionally a comment or question would arise, but most it was uneventful. Jerry was beginning to relax. Maybe it would be all right. Maybe it would all be forgotten. Just as he was finishing his dessert of chocolate pudding, scraping the last bit from the corners of the dish, his mother said, "Angie, you run along. Daddy and I want to talk to Jerry right now. " Angie smiled and said out of the corner of her mouth to Jerry, "You're in for it now." Jerry wanted to punch her in the mouth.

Jerry's father looked up at Jerry and his wife. "So. What seems to be the problem? Or is this going to be good news tonight?" Jerry's mother hesitated and then leaned across to the counter. In her hand was Jerry's reported card which she passed to her husband. He looked at it for what seemed like an eternity and then turned to Jerry. Jerry could feel his father's eyes on him, but he couldn't bring himself to look up. If there were a hole in the floor he would have been happy to slide into it and be gone forever.

"Well Jer, what have you got to say for yourself? This is about the worst report card I've ever seen. You know how much your mother and I want the best for you. But if you don't try hard you make it very difficult for us to help you. It won't be but a few more years and you will want to go to college. You need the best grades you can get. You are making your mother and I very unhappy. How can we be happy if we know you are not trying?" And on it went, his father's voice growing louder and then softer and then louder again. The same words he had heard before were said again. Jerry knew them by heart He knew his parents loved him, but he was also sure that everything he did made them unhappy. They always said so. Jerry sunk lower in his chair. Guilt weighed heavily on him with frustration and despair running a close second and third. "Well, we only have one thing to say Jerry. No bike for two weeks, and those grades had better be good next time." With that his father and mother rose from the table and left him alone. He could hear them talking in low tones in the living room before they put on the television.

"Wow! No bike for two weeks. How am I going to get to baseball practice? Boy is it going to be a long two weeks." The punishment was worse than he had expected. Jerry's mood sunk even lower. He went upstairs and sat on his bed. Even his favorite television program couldn't get his mind off his problems.

SOME THINGS TO THINK ABOUT

1. Do your parents lecture you, and what are you feeling when they do?

2. What kinds of punishments do your parents give you?

3. How do you react when you are punished?

Chapter 3

The next day was cloudy. Rain was in the air and as Jerry woke he knew there would be no baseball practice this afternoon. Groggily he rose from bed and began to dress and wash for school. His mother served breakfast in silence. This was not a surprise. The silent treatment was the usual punishment from his mother. Grabbing his books and sweater, Jerry ran out the front door racing for the school bus which would pick him up at the corner.

There was a group of five boys and girls Jerry's age waiting for the bus. Most of them were talking to each other in groups of twos and threes. But off to one side was Gil. Gil was small for his age. He had dark wavy hair which he wore longer than any of the other boys. Although it was still chilly in the morning, Gil wore only a while "t" shirt with his jeans. Gil had trouble getting along with most of the other boys and usually stayed by himself. Today he seemed to be in a particularly surly mood.

As Jerry passed Gil, Gil called out, "Watch where you're going bean pole. You almost stepped on my books!" Jerry wasn't in the best of moods either and just said, "Oh, go bug off!"

"Oh yeah, beanpole? Who's going to make me?" Gil obviously was not going to let Jerry's remark go by. Jerry turned toward Gil. He could feel his muscles tensing and his stomach knotting. Anger and frustration which had buried itself all night rose in Jerry. All the guilt he had felt from the night before was too much for him to hold any more. Here was a perfect target to release it at. Gil was looking for trouble. So Jerry decided he would help him out, and give him as much as he wanted.

Just then the school bus turned the corner and the other kids began scrambling to be first on board. Gil and Jerry turned their attention toward the bus and then picked up their books. As Jerry began to climb the step into the bus Gil pushed ahead, "Out of my way beanpole!" Jerry just knew he was going to have to punch Gil out. It had gone too far now, but the bus driver had strict rules. Jerry and Gil were forced to sit away from each other during the ride to school. Before they got off the bus though, Jerry heard Gil saying to another boy, "Beanpole has been asking for it. And I'm going to give it to him after school." It was settled then. Jerry and Gil would fight it out this afternoon. The day became as black as the clouds which were massing on the horizon.

As Jerry climbed down from the bus he could feel a dozen sets of eyes on him. He knew that he was trapped into fighting Gil. His reputation and self-esteem seemed to be at stake now. Why couldn't he not worry about what the other kids said? But Jerry felt their thoughts about him were important. How could he walk through the school corridors with his head high if he didn't show what a man he was? He was sure trapped. Now that he had cooled down he realized that he was frightened. Gil might be small but he was strong and wiry. He also had a reputation for fighting dirty. Jerry didn't want to get hurt, but he didn't want to look like a coward or a fool. "I sure am trapped," he thought again.

As the day wore on, Jerry had trouble keeping up with his schoolwork. His mind was wandering back to the night before and the anger and disappointment his parents had felt, and then forward again to the afternoon when he would have to fight it out with Gil. Even his teacher noticed his absentmindedness. "Jerry, buckle down and get your work done. It would seem that you would be working even harder after that report card I had to send home with you yesterday. If this continues I will have no recourse but to fail you. It's about time you shaped up." Even his teacher seemed to be on his back. Jerry's depression thickened and his fear began to grow. He had always tried to be good student. But somehow numbers always seemed to give him problems. They never added up the same way twice. And now math was a monstrous mystery deciphered only by scientists and experts. His parents wanted him to be good at everything, And it seemed he was good at nothing.

On and on his mind wandered. Each thought digging Jerry deeper into fear, guilt and depression. Soon it was three o'clock. Jerry's heart beat loudly in his chest and he swallowed hard. Now he had to face Gil on the bus going home while all his friends watched. If Jerry could have walked home, he would have. If he could have floated away on a cloud never to be seen again, he would have been very happy. But not so. The bus was waiting for him as he left the school door. He was the last one on the bus and Gil was waiting for him.

As Jerry entered the bus, he felt everyone's eyes on him. Gil watched from his seat in the rear of the bus. As Jerry looked at him, Gil began to punch his fist into the palm of his other hand, again and again. Jerry stood for a minute just starring at Gil. The bus driver closed the door, looked back and said, "Okay Let's sit down so I can get you home."

Jerry sat down three rows in front of Gil. He seemed to be surrounded by the noise on the bus—prison walls of sounds. On his back he could feel Gil's eyes. All Jerry's fears, guilt and anxiety began to build until he felt he would explode. As the bus reached his stop Gil rose and left quickly through the door at the front. Jerry gathered his books and followed.

Jerry stepped down and saw Gil waiting for him, his hands on his hips, a smile on his face. The explosion inside Jerry burst out and Gil seemed at that moment to be the cause of all his problems. Fear became anger and he hated

Gil.

Jerry threw his books on the ground and then lunged at Gil. Gil was ready for him and they came together in a bear hug, arms swinging in the hopes of hitting a solid blow. They staggered and fell on the ground in a heap. Jerry's elbows and knees became scraped and bloody. Gil landed a good punch on Jerry's cheek and the pain shot up into his eyes. Jerry's rage began to change into frantic despair, the pain and frustration bringing tears to his eyes. With a cry Jerry grabbed Gil's hair and began to push his face onto the ground.

At that moment Jerry felt someone grab him by the arm and knee and lift him up. Jerry felt himself fall on his side away from Gil. A large teenage boy stood between them. "Okay you guys. You both proved your point. Now get on home. You're both a mess." Gil grabbed his books, took one last look at Jerry and began walking home. Jerry, breathing heavily, could still feel the pain and frustration of the fight, but was very grateful to this boy for stopping them.

"You okay?" he asked Jerry. Jerry nodded and quickly picked up his books. The teenager waved and called to Jerry, "Watch your step kid," and turned the other way, while Jerry began to walk home. Jerry's shirt and pants were torn. Grass stains were on his back, his knees and elbows were bloody. Jerry quietly entered his house. He washed and bandaged his scrapes, stuffed his torn clothes down the bottom of the old toy box in his closet, then lay down on his bed. He could hold in the tears no longer and he cried, deep sobs coming from his throat. Over and over he said to himself, "I need help. Oh, I need help. I'm a mess and I mess everything up. Please somebody, I need help!" The room became darker as the day began to end. And soon Jerry slept.

SOME THINGS TO THINK ABOUT

1. Have you ever had an "enemy?" Who was it and why was he an enemy?

2. When do you feel that the opinions of the other kids are important, and how does this affect what you do?

3. Have you ever been in a fight? What was it like and how did you feel about it?

Chapter 4

The sun began sneaking through a space under the bottom of the window shade in Jerry's room. He could hear a lawn mower somewhere down the block. Jerry opened his eyes and stared at the window. Saturday -- the first happy thought of the day for Jerry.

"Well," he said to himself. "No school today and there's baseball practice this afternoon. I think this day is gonna be better than yesterday!" And Jerry was feeling better. His scrapes felt only a little stiff. His Mom and Dad hadn't asked about the bandaids on his elbows. And baseball practice was always fun. The fears and frustrations of yesterday seemed to have disappeared overnight with the clouds and Jerry's spirits were as bright as the sun.

As Jerry went down to breakfast a small thought tickled his mind and then went away. "I did ask for help last night, and today is sure better. Maybe asking helped!"

Breakfast tasted good and the chores for Saturday morning were finished quickly and easily. Soon it was lunchtime and Jerry was off to baseball practice. Jerry decided not to feel annoyed about not having his bike for two weeks. Today was nice and the walk to practice would only take fifteen minutes.

The coach, Mr. Jameson, was already lining up the boys on Jerry's team and giving them places on the field, when Jerry walked up. "Go over there with Will. He is going to take you over to the other side of the field to practice pitching."

Jerry followed Mr. Jameson's pointing finger and then stopped. Will was standing next to another boy. He was showing him how to grip the baseball. The boy was looking down at Will's hand and neither of them noticed Jerry standing and staring. Will was a tall teenager, obviously Mr. Jameson's son, for he had the coach's red hair and freckles. But the surprise was in Jerry's recognition of Will. He was the fellow who had stopped the fight only yesterday. But the surprise didn't stop there. The new pitcher watching Will's fingers on the ball was also known to Jerry. In fact, he could still feel the soreness on his cheek from the pitcher's fist. It was Gil.

Jerry didn't know what to do, but was saved from making a decision by Will's voice. Looking up from the ball Will noticed Jerry and called, "Well, look who's here. Come on over and join us."

Just then a cloud covered the sun, chilling the air and Jerry's spirits dropped with the temperature. "Hi there. You must be Jerry, our star pitcher. I'm Will. It seems we met yesterday...and I guess you and Gil know each other already," Will added with chuckle. "Gil is going to be your relief pitcher."

The two boys glared at each other while Will watched them closely. No more was the day bright and clear. Jerry saw before him what he again thought to be the cause of all his problems. Gil was the menace in his life and Gil was the enemy. Anger grew inside of Jerry. He didn't ask himself why he saw Gil this way. He only knew his own anger, and Gil seemed to be the perfect target. If he could just send all of that anger out at Gil perhaps he, Jerry, could be rid of all his fear, his worries and his problems.

Almost as if Jerry could read Gil's mind he saw the same thoughts about himself in Gil's eyes. "All the more reason to hate him," thought Jerry. "Since Gil doesn't like me any more than I like him, I'll just have to prove I'm better. I'm not a mess—he is!"

Gently, but firmly Will gained the boys' attention and began working with them. First Jerry would throw the ball and Gil would act as catcher. Then they would reverse positions. And so it continued for the next hour.

"Okay guys. Practice is over for now. You're both doing fine. In fact you are throwing the ball so hard you'd think you wanted to kill each other," he added with a twinkle in his eyes. "See you next Monday for practice."

As Will passed Jerry, he heard Jerry mumbling, "Why did he have to be my relief? Boy, what a rotten break!" Jerry began kicking the dirt with his sneaker. Will put a hand on his shoulder and looked in Jerry's eyes. Will's eyes were clear and blue and friendly. "There are no accidents kid! You guys are meant for each other!" And then he laughed, ruffling the hair on the top of Jerry's head before he turned and left.

"Now what does that mean?" Jerry thought with annoyance.

SOME THINGS TO THINK ABOUT

1. Think about a recent argument or fight you have had. Was the other person a target for your pent-up anger and fear? Did the fight get rid of your anger and fear?

2. Have you ever had someone older help you out when you needed it? Who was it and how did they help you?

3. What do you think Will meant by, "There are no accidents kid!"?

Chapter 5

The rest of the weekend was uneventful. Soon it was Monday. Jerry was up, ate breakfast and was off to the bus stop early. But not early enough, for Gil was already there waiting. Jerry stopped a distance away and refused to look at Gil. He could sense Gil doing the same thing. Jerry slowly walked to the open door of the bus so Gil would have plenty of time to get to his seat without bumping into Jerry. He just didn't feel like getting into trouble today.

"I'll just keep my distance from Gil," thought Jerry. "Then for today at least I won't have any problems." But still inside of Jerry there was a tight knot of pain. Whether it was anger or fear didn't seem to matter, it simply hurt. But Jerry decided not to look at it too closely. Jerry followed the same plan for the rest of the school day. Whenever his teacher came near to see how he was doing, Jerry moved to another job or place in the room. The pain was still strong inside of him, but Jerry still didn't want to look at it. He just kept moving away from what he thought were his problems.

That afternoon Jerry found himself walking to baseball practice. The pain was getting stronger each time he thought about walking instead of riding his bike, but Jerry stuffed the thoughts back down inside him. The knot in his stomach got tighter.

Will was waiting for him when he got to the field and Jerry felt better. Will always had a smile on his face and a friendly hand to help him. Will grinned and said, "Looks like it will be just the two of us. Gil is going to be late."

The relief on Jerry's face was so clear that Will asked, "What's with you two? There's never any reason to hate someone like you two hate each other. In fact there's never any reason to hate anyone. Most of the time hate means you don't know what is really happening. You get scared and decide the only way to handle it is to get angry at somebody else. Then maybe whatever the problem is will be his fault and not your own."

Jerry thought about Will's comments. He had to be honest with himself. Had Gil really done anything to him? Or had Gil been a good target for all of Jerry's fears when he didn't know how to handle them?

" I think you may be right, Will," Jerry said turning pink with guilt and embarrassment. "But what can I do now? Gil is still angry with me. How can I protect myself?" Jerry added, sticking out his chin as if to say...now answer this one smarty! But Will just smiled gently and said, "There is another way of handling problems kid. You don't have to fight and you don't have to run away."

Jerry looked him in disbelief. What else could you possibly do, he thought? As if Will could read his mind he answered him, "You look for the peaceful answer inside yourself. All the answers you could ever need are right inside of you. You don't even need to ask anyone else what to do. You will know what's right. It will just feel good when you think about it!" But Will added a warning, "Remember, there's a trick to doing this. Don't try to figure out what the answer should be, just let it float into you mind. You see, kid, your own thinking and scheming has gotten you into this mess. You need Bigger Help than your own schemes to get you out."

"Now wait a minute," Jerry interrupted. "First you tell me the answer is inside of my head. Then you tell me not to listen to my own thinking. Well who the heck does give me the answer," Jerry demanded!

Just then Gil walked up. But Jerry noticed Gil didn't just walk, he swaggered, and his eyes told Jerry he still had it in for him. For a moment Jerry felt his anger rise, and then he remember what Will had said. "But I don't know what to do?" Jerry thought, and suddenly, almost as if a light bulb went on in his head, Jerry decided to offer Gil his glove to borrow for practice. Gil's was old and too small, while Jerry's was the right size and just softened up enough. Jerry knew how good it felt to use his glove and knew it would help Gil catch better. Before Jerry thought about it any more he found himself saying, "Hi Gil. Maybe you want to borrow my glove for practice. It's really super!" And Jerry felt good inside.

Gil stared at Jerry and then at the glove. Very slowly a smile played at the corners of his mouth and then he said quietly, "Gee, that would be great. " As he tried on the glove his smile broadened and he added. "Hey, Jerry, thanks. This is great!" And Jerry felt even better inside.

"You know," he thought to himself. "Maybe there is another way." But then he wasn't sure. Would it work all the time? And where did that thought come from? Jerry knew he had never planned to say that to Gil, and yet, he sure felt good!

SOME THINGS TO THINK ABOUT

1. Have you ever tried to make believe you don't have to fix your problems, and you tried to avoid them instead? What happened to your fear and anger when you did this?
2. When have you tried to think peaceful thoughts instead of unhappy thoughts? What happened when you did?

Chapter 6

As Jerry got back to the house he saw Angie on the front lawn. She was trailing her kite behind her, running as fast as she could. The wind was barely lifting the kite off the ground and as she tried to get the kite to lift she would let out more string. As Jerry watched, Angie stopped, let the kite fall to the ground, and began to pull in the extra string toward herself. Now Jerry could see what the problem was. She didn't roll the string neatly around a stick. She just pulled it together into a tangled ball.

"Angie," Jerry called. "Let me help you with that kite."

Angie looked up at Jerry suspiciously. The last time she had talked to him about the kite he had told her to bug off. The mess was her's to clean up.

Jerry could read her thoughts across her face and said, "Look Angie. I'm sorry I yelled last time. I just had a lot of problems on my mind. I can show you how to keep that string from tangling," he added helpfully.

"Oh that's okay," said Angie. And then she smiled and to Jerry the whole world filled with sunlight. She looked up at him with so much thanks that Jerry felt ten feet tall. He gently took the string, began winding it around a stick and showed Angie how to do it neatly.

"Now the string will roll out smoothly for you. And when you roll it back up it won't get tangled."

Jerry turned and went up the driveway toward the side door. "Maybe there is a better way to do things without anger and guilt," Jerry thought. Jerry kept remembering the smile on Angie's face when he offered to help rather than to hurt. And he sure did feel good about it.

As he got to the door he noticed a strange car in the driveway. "I wonder who is visiting Mom and Dad?" Jerry thought. As he stepped into the hallway he found out. His heart skipped a beat and a cold chill of fear filled his stomach. His teacher was sitting in the living room with his mother and father. They were drinking coffee, and as they heard Jerry come in his mother called, "Jerry will you please join us? We would like to talk to you. "

Slowly Jerry walked into the room and sat on the corner of the couch, as far away from everyone as he could get. "I knew this couldn't last!" Jerry thought. "Everything was going too well." For no reason that Jerry could understand Will's face filled his mind. He could even hear Will say, "There are no accidents kid...there's always a better way of doing things...." So Jerry tried it once more and thought, "I need help. I don't want to be afraid. I do want to be good at school and make my parents feel good about me. Now how do I do that?"

No sooner had he placed his request for help into his mind, then he heard his father say, "Jerry we are all here to help you. We know you are afraid and we don't want you to feel that way. We know you can be good at school, and we want to help you do that. Your mother and I love you and your teacher is here because she wants to help."

Wow! That was quick service, thought Jerry. Jerry's heart lifted. He took another good look at his parents and his teacher. They were here to help him and they were all truly worried about him. Jerry saw all three of them in a different light. All the nagging was just another way of saying, "We love you. We are concerned about you."

"Hey, thanks," said Jerry. "I think I really do need the help. I want to try to do the right thing." And for the next half hour the four of them sat and planned a study schedule that fit around baseball practice and play time. Jerry began to feel really great.

Later on that night as Jerry lay on his bed he thought, "Just maybe there is another way to handle problems. All I did was say "help" and sure enough help was on the way. First Will, then my parents, and even Gil and Angie helped with their smiles. Will said it came from inside of me, but I could also see it inside of everyone else. You know, this world is really fun to be in. I can't wait to see Will again and talk to him about this.

"Wow! Talk about quick service! Help was on the way as soon as I asked for it!"

SOME THINGS TO THINK ABOUT

1. How do other people react when you try to be helpful?

2. When you are honest and apologize, how do you feel and how do others react?

3. Do you think Jerry's asking for help, and then getting it can happen for you if you try it?

Chapter 7

All Monday went great for Jerry. Whenever he got worried or angry he asked for help. And sure enough his mind would tell him what to say or do that was truly helpful and always made him feel good . Many times to his surprise other people would almost immediately give him the help or the answer he needed even before he could think of it himself. And for the rest of the day Jerry tried very hard to remember to ask for help whenever he didn't feel good about anything.

That afternoon Jerry rode down to baseball practice on his bike. His parents were so pleased with his attitude about the new study program they removed all punishments about his report card. Jerry felt great.

There was Will, waiting for him. Gil hadn't gotten there yet so Jerry decided now was a good time to talk to Will. He wanted to know why things were going so well. Did he simply have to ask for help and he would get it? Gee, there were so many questions that needed answers, all exciting. Jerry just knew that whatever Will told him was going to be of help to him, maybe for the rest of his life.

Jerry jumped sideways off his bike and let it fall into the dirt as he practically ran up to Will. "Will, you'll never guess what happened! The last three days have been super. I've been trying to look at things just the way you said. And boy, have strange things been happening. But Will," Jerry asked, "Is this really happening? Or am I just imagining things? Hey Will, what's going on?"

Will's face crinkled into a smile and then he threw his head back and laughed. "This is great, Jerry." Will said. "I knew you would think about things twice. Let's sit down over here under the tree and talk for awhile. I've got some things I want to share with you. "

For the next hour or so Will and Jerry sat with heads bowed talking quietly with each other. As Will picked a piece of grass and placed it in his mouth to suck on, he began to talk.

"When I was your age I was the meanest kid on my street. The only way I talked to people was with a sneer on my face. I was so frightened of everyone and everything I knew I had better build up a good defense to keep problems away. I yelled and then I would get silent. My parents started to yell right back at me. My teachers started throwing me out of the classroom because I was always causing trouble. "

"Boy," said Jerry with wonder in his eyes. "I wouldn't have believed it. You always seem so calm and friendly."

"Well, I wasn't always like this. In fact, sometimes I still get real scared and angry and I have to remember just what I told you. You see, someone a little older than me talked to me just the way I talked to you.

"He told me there was a better way of handling things. Oh, I wasn't as quick as you were to try it. Oh no. I thought I was smarter and could do it better myself. But when I noticed that I was losing friends left and right, that I was angry with everyone and everything and that I hurt inside all the time, I finally realized I would try anything to feel better! And so, just like you I asked for help, and sure enough I found it."

"But what is it we're really doing?" asked Jerry.

And Will continued, "Inside of us are all the answers we could possibly need. Its Love, Jerry. I call it God. He is in you, around you and in everyone and everything. You and everything are joined by this Love because this is the Home and Family we all really belong to.

"When we get frightened and angry what we are really saying is that we don't want to be a part of this Family. We put up walls around us to keep us 'safe'. And you know what happens?"

"Oh, I can answer that," replied Jerry. "I feel more alone and frightened, and then I want to blame everyone else for the pain I feel. When I felt like that, I was building more walls with my yelling and fighting. It sure didn't make me feel any better!"

"We've all been there before, Jerry." added Will. "And you know what? We will try that way of handling things again. Boy, do we get stubborn. But we have to keep remembering that the Help is in us and around us because God loves us. And that Love is in everyone binding us all together like glue. Yup, when you think you are alone you couldn't be further from the truth."

As Jerry watched, Will pulled some paper from his backpack which he laid next to him on the grass. Will said, "Here's something for you to look at. This is what helped me and I wrote it down because I just knew you would want to know more. " Will handed Jerry a stack of papers, neatly typed, and stapled together in a corner.

"These are your copies, Jerry," Will said. "Look at them, read them, and try to follow them very carefully. I can guarantee you that if you want to feel better, this will do it! This is a way to get in touch with the part of you that does know it All! Buddy, it's the best gift I could ever give you."

As Jerry looked at the pages and then into Will's eyes he just knew that the Answer was with him now. Jerry's heart thumped, and for a reason he couldn't understand, tears of joy began to smart in his eyes. Jerry blinked them back fast. He wasn't going to start acting liked a baby now. After all, he knew this was the first big step in growing up, and he wanted to do it right.

As Will smiled at Jerry, Jerry smile back. At the same time they stuck out their hands and shook. A new life was beginning for Jerry.

Later that night, Jerry sat up in bed. It was past his bedtime and his mother had made him turn the lights off in his room. But under the covers Jerry held a flashlight. Slowly he turned to the first page and began to read Will's typing....

WILL'S GUIDE TO BETTER LIVING
(Use this whenever you don't feel happy)

DO I LIKE WHAT I'M FEELING?

Remember, kid, you're not trapped. If don't feel good; if you're worried, scared, angry, guilty embar-rassed, sad -- there is a way out of it. You can find the answer, and you can feel good. But do you want to?

CAN I SEE THIS DIFFERENTLY?

Take a moment and look for something good in the situation you are in. Is there anything about your situation that can make you feel good, and begin to give you the answer you need? If you find it, you're feeling better already and you're on the right track.

IF NOT, DO I REALLY WANT TO SEE THIS DIFFERENTLY?

If you can't find any good, it's because you're holding onto your bad feeling because, inside you think it will get you something you want. Remember, the only thing it's getting you is a bad feeling. So decide again -- do you want to see this differently?

THERE IS SOMETHING INSIDE ME THAT CAN SHOW ME THE WAY.

You are never alone. God's Love is in your mind ready to show you the way and make you feel good. God's Love is in everyone's mind so His Answer will always be right for you and everyone else!

DO I WANT TO BE SHOWN THE WAY?

This is it, kid. Do you want to let go of your anger, guilt, sadness and let Love guide you? Or do you want to be stubborn and continue to have more pain? It's your choice.

I WILL BE STILL AND LET THE ANSWER COME.

Stop trying to figure things out. Admit you don't

know the answer and take a big step in growing up. Let the Voice which knows the Answer guide you. Let it slip into your mind. Maybe you'll hear your mind telling you what to do; maybe you'll get an idea; or maybe you'll just feel good and know everything is all right. But remember, the Answer always makes you feel good!

Jerry saw that Will had handwritten something on the page:

> *"This always helped me. I guarantee it will help you. Remember, kid, if you are not feeling good start with step one again until your mind is quiet, the answer comes and you feel good!"*

Jerry already felt good. He carefully put Will's notes away and he fell sound asleep. The next morning, before he got out of bed he began to read the next pages. And from then on, every day he followed what they said. The pages started this way....

WILL'S WAY TO LISTEN AND LIVE
(A one year program for growing up happy)

WEEK 1
Every morning repeat this line: "I want only to feel good, and I can!"

Remember to use WILL'S GUIDE FOR BETTER LIVING whenever you are stuck in a bad feeling.

WEEK 2
Every morning repeat this line: "Goodness is my right and everybody else's right too!"

Remember to use WILL'S GUIDE FOR BETTER LIVING whenever you are stuck in a bad feeling.

WEEK 3
Sit for a moment and look at all the things in your room and say to yourself why you feel good about them. For example: "What a great room I have," or "What a neat pair of sneakers I have on." (Just a few things will do.)

Remember to use WILL'S GUIDE FOR BETTER LIVING whenever you are stuck in a bad feeling

WEEK 4
Sit for a moment, close your eyes and think about the home you live in, the school you go to, the places you play at and say to yourself why you feel good about them. For example: "What a great house I live in, it makes me feel good," or "I have lots of nice places to play. I'm lucky." (Just a few will do.)

Remember to use WILL'S GUIDE FOR BETTER LIVING whenever you are stuck in a bad feeling.

WEEK 5
Sit for a moment, close your eyes and see some of the people in your life. Let them come to your mind one my one. Find something good about each one and say, for example: "Mom cooks my favorite food," or "Dad gives the best hugs," or "My teacher always helps me."

Remember to use WILL'S GUIDE FOR BETTER LIVING whenever you are stuck in a bad feeling.

WEEK 6
Repeat this phrase in the morning and before you sleep at night. "I have only loving people around me."

Remember to use WILL'S GUIDE FOR BETTER LIVING whenever you are stuck in a bad feeling.

WEEK 7
Repeat this phrase in the morning and before you sleep at night. "I am always protected."

Remember to use WILL'S GUIDE FOR BETTER LIVING whenever you are stuck in a bad feeling.

WEEK 8
Repeat this phrase in the morning and at bedtime: "I am surrounded by Love."

Remember to use WILL'S GUIDE FOR BETTER LIVING whenever you

are stuck in a bad feeling.

WEEK 9
Repeat this phrase in the morning and at bedtime: "Everything in my life are gifts of love to me and I choose to see them."

Remember to use WILL'S GUIDE FOR BETTER LIVING whenever you are stuck in a bad feeling.

WEEK 10
It's time to look more closely at those gifts of love. Sit quietly in the morning and let the gifts appear in your mind. Then say to yourself something like this for each one, "I recognize the love my mother gives me," or "I recognize the safe home I live in."

Remember to use WILL'S GUIDE FOR BETTER LIVING whenever you are stuck in a bad feeling.

WEEK 11
Sit quietly and look again at the lovely gifts you receive. This time pick someone who seems to make you feel bad. Remember WILL'S GUIDE and decide to see this person differently. When you feel good about the people around you, you feel good about yourself.

DON'T TRY TO FIGURE THIS OUT. Just let the nice thoughts about this person slip into your mind.

WEEK 12
Repeat this in the morning and at bedtime and AT LEAST ONCE MORE during the day, "Love is inside, of me, outside of me, in fact it IS me, and I feel good."

Remember WILL'S GUIDE.

WEEK 13
Ask this question in the morning, at bedtime and once during the day AND WAIT FOR THE ANSWER THAT MAKES YOU FEEL GOOD: "Where does the love which IS ME, come from?"

Remember WILL'S GUIDE.

WEEK 14
Repeat this phrase in the morning, at bedtime and once during the day, "God's Love makes me happy and makes me safe."

Remember WILL'S GUIDE.

WEEK 15
Sit quietly in the morning and listen with your mind for God's Voice. What will it be like? Only you will know because it will be just for you, and His Answer will make you feel good. Take your time, there is no rush. And if you are careful you will be able to hear God's Voice in your friends, in your family, and even on the TV. His Answer always makes you feel good.

Remember WILL'S GUIDE.

WEEK 16
Repeat this phrase as often as you like all day. "I hear God's Voice in me and around me. It makes me feel good."

Remember WILL'S GUIDE.

WEEK 17
Repeat this phrase morning, midday and night. "God loves me and I love Him."

Remember WILL'S GUIDE.

WEEK 18
Repeat this phrase, morning, midday and night. "God loves me and gives me loving things."
Remember WILL'S GUIDE.

WEEK 19
Repeat this phrase morning, midday, and night. "God loves me and surrounds me with loving people."

Remember WILL'S GUIDE.

WEEK 20
Repeat this morning, midday and night. "I am God's child, and

so is the whole world! I choose to see God's Love everywhere."

Remember WILL'S GUIDE.

WEEK 21
Repeat this morning, midday and night: "How does God want me to see all things?"

Remember WILL'S GUIDE.

WEEK 22
Repeat this phrase throughout the day: "What would God have me say to all things today?"

Remember WILL'S GUIDE.

WEEK 23
Repeat this phrase throughout the day: "What would God have me do today?"

Remember WILL'S GUIDE.

WEEK 24
Repeat this phrase throughout the day: "When I do God's Will I do my own, and I feel good!"

Remember WILL'S GUIDE.

WEEK 25
Repeat this phrase throughout the day: "I will learn from everything around me. And true learning always makes me feel good."

Remember WILL'S GUIDE.

WEEK 26
Repeat this phrase throughout the day: "I will listen to, look at and learn from everything around me."

Remember WILL'S GUIDE.

WEEK 27
Sit quietly in the morning and let family and friends come to mind. As each one appears in your mind, let God's Voice show you the goodness in each of them. As you see their goodness you will know your own.

Remember WILL'S GUIDE.

WEEK 28
Sit quietly in the morning and let all your problems come to mind. As each one appears say, "I will let God's Voice show me the truth and my problem will be solved. Truth always makes me feel good!"

Remember WILL'S GUIDE.

WEEK 29
Repeat this phrase whenever you need to: "God's Voice solves all my problems."

Remember WILL'S GUIDE.

WEEK 30
Repeat this phrase whenever necessary: "I am God's child and He always helps me!"

Remember WILL'S GUIDE.

WEEK 31
Repeat this phrase whenever necessary: "God's Voice shows me what to say and what to do so I can feel good."

Remember WILL'S GUIDE.

WEEK 32
Repeat this phrase whenever necessary: "God's Love is my love and everyone's love."

Remember WILL'S GUIDE.

WEEK 33
"Today I take the time to love." Think of this all day long.

Remember WILL'S GUIDE.

WEEK 34
"Today is my chance to be of help. And helping makes me feel great!" Think of this all day long.

Remember WILL'S GUIDE.

WEEK 35
Sit quietly today and tell each person you can think of that he is great. They need to know this, and your thoughts WILL touch them.

Remember WILL'S GUIDE.

WEEK 36
Let only good thoughts be in your mind this week. Whenever you don't feel right, STOP. Remember WILL'S GUIDE FOR BETTER LIVING and then say, "I only want happiness." NOW LOOK FOR IT.

WEEK 37
"This week my hopes are heard." Now listen to God's Voice in everything around you.

Remember WILL'S GUIDE.

WEEK 38
"I am whole and happy. The world loves me. If you feel unloved remember WILL'S GUIDE, and don't waste any time!

WEEK 39
Sit quietly each morning and let Love open your mind. See how creative you can be. Say often, "I am open to everything."

Remember WILL'S GUIDE.

WEEK 40
"God's Love is in me and around me. I want to see It. It makes me feel good."

Remember WILL'S GUIDE.

WEEK 41
"The Light of Wisdom guides my life. And if I need to know anything, I will be given the Answer."

Remember WILL'S GUIDE.

WEEK 42.
"The time I take to listen to Love will always make me feel good."

Remember WILL'S GUIDE.

WEEK 43
Sit quietly and let each problem come to your mind. Don't think long about them! Simply say, "I give this problem to God's Voice Who will make everything right."

Remember WILL'S GUIDE.

WEEK 44
"Help is on the way! All I need do is watch and listen for it."

Remember WILL'S GUIDE.

WEEK 45
"Today I will help everyone, because I know it helps me feel good, too! God's Voice will tell me how to help."

Remember WILL'S GUIDE.

WEEK 46
"I want only peace." "I want only happiness." "I want only to help." "I want only God's help." And here it comes!

Remember WILL'S GUIDE.

WEEK 47
"This is the week I grow inside. And everyone is proud

of me."

Remember WILL'S GUIDE.

WEEK 48
"This is the week I help everyone grow inside. God's Voice will show me how to help."

Remember WILL'S GUIDE.

WEEK 49
"I am surrounded by good!"

Remember WILL'S GUIDE.

WEEK 50
"The world is a great place to be. Only God's love is here."

Remember WILL'S GUIDE.

WEEK 51
"I am surrounded by great people. I love them."

Remember WILL'S GUIDE.

WEEK 52
Sit quietly and remember this year. The good and the bad. Now look at how much more good you are able to see.

And Jerry did his weekly lessons, remembering to use WILL'S GUIDE FOR BETTER LIVING each time he got stuck in bad feelings. At the end of the year he had formed some really good habits. When he got angry, sad or worried he thought about his lesson for that day and week and God's Voice helped him. Sometimes he heard the Answer in his mind, sometimes he got the answer from parents or friends, and sometimes the person he was angry with gave him the right answer. And Jerry always felt good.

At the end of the typed pages Will had written the following words:

"Help is on the way, and here it comes now!
Enjoy the rest of your life."

And the last page was signed,

"Love, Will"